UP IN MAINE

TO MY FRIEND
AND FELLOW IN THE CRAFT OF LETTERS
WINFIELD M. THOMPSON
TO WHOM I AM INDEBTED
FOR MORE THAN ONE OF THE STORIES
TOLD HEREIN
THIS VOLUME IS DEDICATED

PREFACE

I don't know how to weave a roundelay,
   I couldn't voice a sighing song of love;
No mellow lyre that on which I play;
   I plunk a strident lute without a glove.

The rhythm that is running through my stuff
   Is not the whisp of maiden's trailing gown;
The metre, maybe, gallops rather rough,
   Like river-drivers storming down to town.

—It's more than likely something from the
      wood,
   Where chocking axes scare the deer and
      moose;
A homely rhyme, and easy understood
   — An echo from the weird domain of Spruce.

Or else it's just some Yankee notion, dressed
   In rough-and-ready "Uncle Dudley" phrase;
Some honest thought we common folks suggest,
   — Some tricksy mem'ry-flash from boyhood's
      days.

I cannot polish off this stilted rhyme
   With all these homely notions in my brain.
A sonnet, sir, would stick me every time;
   Let's have a chat 'bout common things in
      Maine.

HOLMAN F. DAY.

CONTENTS

CONTENTS

INTRODUCTION

ABOUT three thousand years ago the "Preacher" declared that "of making many books there is no end." This sublimely pessimistic truism deserves to be considered in connection with the time when it was written; otherwise it might accomplish results not intended by its author.

It must be remembered that in the "Preacher's" time books were altogether in writing. It should also be borne in mind that if the handwriting which we have in these days, speaking of the period prior to the advent of the female typewriter, is to be accepted as any criterion, — and inasmuch as all concede that history repeats itself, that may well be assumed, — it is easy to understand how, by reason of its illegibility, he was also led to declare that "much study is a weariness of the flesh." It is quite obvious that this was the moving cause of his delightfully doleful utterance as to books. Had he lived in this year nineteen hundred, at either the closing of the nineteenth or the dawning of the twentieth century, — as to whether it is closing or dawning I make no assertion,

— he might well have made the same criticism, but from an optimistic standpoint.

A competent litterateur informs me that there are now extant 3,725,423,201 books; that in America and England alone during the last year 12,888 books entered upon a precarious existence, with the faint though unexpressed hope of surviving "life's fitful fever." If the conditions of the "Preacher's" time obtained to-day, the vocabulary of pessimism would be inadequate for the expression of similar views.

A careful examination by the writer, of all these well-nigh innumerable monuments of learning, discloses the fact that the work now being introduced to what I trust may be an equally innumerable army of readers has no parallel in literature. If justification were needed, that fact alone justifies its existence. This fact, however, is not necessary, as the all-sufficient fact which warrants the collection of these unique sketches in book form is that no one can read them without being interested, entertained, and amused, as well as instructed and improved. "The stubborn strength of Plymouth Rock" is nowhere better exemplified than on the Maine farm, in the Maine woods, on the Maine coast, or in the Maine workshop. From them the author of "Up in Maine" has drawn his inspiration. Rugged independence, singleness of purpose, unswerving integrity, philosophy adequate for all occasions, the great realities of life, and a cheerful disregard of conventionalities, are here found in all their native strength and vigor. These peculiarities as delineated may be rough, perhaps uncouth, but they are characteristic, picturesque, engaging, and lifelike. His subjects are rough diamonds. They have the inherent qualities from which great characters are developed, and out of which heroes are made.

Through every chink and crevice of these rugged portrayals glitters the sheen of pure gold, gold of standard weight and fineness, "gold tried in the fire." Finally it should be said that this is what is now known as a book with a purpose, and that purpose, as the author confidentially informs me, is to sell as many copies as possible, which he confidently expects to do. To this most worthy end I trust I may have, in a small degree, contributed by this introduction.

C. E. LITTLEFIELD.

Washington, D.C., March 17, 1900.

'ROUND HOME

AUNT SHAW'S PET JUG

Now there was Uncle Elnathan Shaw,
— Most regular man you ever saw !
Just half-past four in the afternoon
He'd start and whistle that old jig tune,
Take the big blue jug from the but'ry shelf
And trot down cellar, to draw himself
Old cider enough to last him through
The winter ev'nin'.   Two quarts would do.
— Just as regular as half-past four
Come round, he'd tackle that cellar door,
As he had for thutty years or more.

And as regular, too, as he took that jug
Aunt Shaw would yap through her old cross
    mug,
" Now, Nathan, for goodness' sake take care !
You allus trip on the second stair ;
It seems as though you were just possessed
To break that jug.   It's the very best
There is in town and you know it, too,
And 'twas left to me by my great-aunt Sue.
For goodness' sake, why don't yer lug
A tin dish down, for ye'll break that jug ? "
Allus the same, suh, for thirty years,
Allus the same old twits and jeers
Slammed for the nineteenth thousand time
And still we wonder, my friend, at crime.

But Nathan took it meek's a pup
And the worst he said was " Please shut up."
You know what the Good Book says befell
The pitcher that went to the old-time well ;
Wal, whether 'twas that or his time had come,
Or his stiff old limbs got weak and numb
Or whether his nerves at last giv' in
To Aunt Shaw's everlasting chin —
One day he slipped on that second stair,
Whirled round and grabbed at the empty air
And clean to the foot of them stairs, ker-smack,
He bumped on the bulge of his humped old back
And he'd hardly finished the final bump
When old Aunt Shaw she giv' a jump
And screamed downstairs as mad's a bug
" Dod-rot your hide, did ye break my jug ? "

Poor Uncle Nathan lay there flat
Knocked in the shape of an old cocked hat,
But he rubbed his legs, brushed off the dirt
And found after all that he warn't much hurt.
And he'd saved the jug, for his last wild thought
Had been of that ; he might have caught
At the cellar shelves and saved his fall,
But he kept his hands on the jug through all.
And now as he loosed his jealous hug
His wife just screamed, " Did ye break my
jug ? "

Not a single word for his poor old bones
Nor a word when she heard his awful groans,
But the blamed old hard-shelled turkle just
Wanted to know if that jug was bust.
Old Uncle Nathan he let one roar
And he shook his fist at the cellar door;
" Did ye break my jug? " she was yellin' still.
" No, durn yer pelt, but I swow I will."
And you'd thought that the house was a-going
　　to fall
When the old jug smashed on the cellar wall.

OLD BOGGS'S SLARNT

Old Bill Boggs is always sayin' that he'd like to
  but he carn't;
He hain't never had no chances, he hain't never
  got no slarnt.
Says it's all dum foolish tryin', 'less ye git the
  proper start,
Says he's never seed no op'nin' so he's never
  had no heart.
But he's chawed enough tobacker for to fill a
  hogset up
And has spent his time a-trainin' some all-fired
  kind of pup;
While his wife has took in washin' and his children hain't been larnt
'Cause old Boggs is allus whinin' that he's never
  got no slarnt.

Them air young uns round the gros'ry hadn't
  oughter done the thing!
Now it's done, though, and it's over, 'twas a
  cracker-jack, by jing.
Boggs, ye see, has been a-settin' twenty years on
  one old plank,
One end h'isted on a saw hoss, t'other on the
  cistern tank.
T'other night he was a-chawin' and he says, "I
  vum-spt-ooo —

Here I am a-owin' money — not a gol durn thing
to do!
'Tain't no use er buckin' chances, ner er fightin'
back at Luck,
— Less ye have some way er startin', feller's
sartin to be stuck.
Needs a slarnt to git yer going" — then them
young uns give a carnt,
— Plank went up an' down old Boggs went —
yas, he got it, got his slarnt.
Course the young uns shouldn't done it — sent
mine off along to bed —
Helped to pry Boggs out the cistern — he warn't
more'n three-quarters dead.
Didn't no one 'prove the actions, but when all
them kids was gone,
Thunder mighty! How we hollered! Gab'rel
couldn't heered his horn.

CY NYE, PREVARICATOR

Cy
  Nye
    Thunder, how he'll lie!
Never has to stop and think — never has to try.
Says he had a settin' hen that acted clean pos-
    sessed;
Says a kag o' powder couldn't shake her off her
    nest;
Didn't mind a flannel rag tied around her tail;
Ev'ry now and then he'd take 'er, souse 'er in
    a pail;
Never had the least effect — feathers even friz;
Then she set and pecked the ice, but 'tended
    right to biz.
'Peared to care for nothin' else 'cept to set and
    set;
Didn't seem to care a tunket what she drunk
    or et.
Cy he said he got so mad he thought he'd use
    'er ha'ash,
So he went to feedin' on 'er hemlock sawdust
    mash.
Hen she gobbled down the stuff, reg'lar as
    could be;
"Reely seemed to fat 'er up," Cy says he to me.
Shows the power of the mind when it gets a
    clutch.

Hen imagined it was bran — helped 'er just as
much.

Then she hid her nest away — laid a dozen eggs ;

'Leven chickens that she hatched all had wooden
legs,

T'other egg it wouldn't hatch — solid junk o'
wood,

Hen's a-wrasslin' with it yet — thinks the thing
is good.

      Thunder, how he'll lie !
        But he's dry,
          — That Cy.

Cy
  Nye
    Tells another lie :

Claims to be the strongest man around here ;
this is why :

Says he bought a side o' beef up to Johnson's store,

Tucked it underneath his arm — didn't mind it
more

Than a pound o' pickled tripe ; sauntered down
the road,

Got to ponderin' Bible texts — clean forgot his
load.

All to once he chanced to think he meant to get
some meat,

Hustled back to Johnson's store t'other end the
street,

Bought another side o' beef. The boys commenced to laugh,
— Vummed he hadn't sensed till then he lugged
the other half.
   Can't deny
    'T he can lie,
     — That Cy.

UNCLE BENJY AND OLD CRANE

Once there was a country lawyer and his name
  was Hiram Crane,
And he had a reputation as the worst old file in
  Maine.
And as soon's he got a client, why, the first
  thing that he'd do
Was to feel the critter's pocket and then soak
  him 'cordin' to.

Well, sir, one day Benjy Butters bought a hoss,
  and oh, 'twas raw
Way old Benjy he got roasted, and he said he'd
  have the law.
So he gave the case to Hiram, and then Hiram
  brought a suit
And got back the hoss and harness and what
  Benjy gave to boot.

When he met him at the gros'ry Benjy asked
  him for the bill,
And when Hiram named the figger, it was
  steeper'n Hobson's hill.
Poor old Benjy hammed and swallered — bill jest
  sort of took his breath,
And the crowd that stood a-listenin' thought
  perhaps he'd choke to death.

But it happened that the squire felt like jokin'
    some that day,
And he says, " Now, Uncle Benjy, there won't be
    a cent to pay
If you'll right here on the instant make me up a
    nice pat rhyme;
Hear you're pretty good at them things — give
    you jest three minutes' time."
And the squire grinned like fury, tipped the
    crowd a knowing wink,
While old Benjy started in, sir, almost 'fore
    you'd time to think:

" Here you see the petty lawyer leanin' on his
    corkscrew cane.
Sartin parties call him Gander, other people call
    him Crane.
Though he's faowl, it's someways daoubtful
    what he is, my friends, but still
You can tell there's hawk about him by the
    gaul-durned critter's bill."

Crane got mad, he wanted money, but the crowd
    let on to roar,
And they laughed the blamed old skinflint right
    square out the gros'ry store.

"PLUG"

For sixty years he had borne the name
  Of "Plug" — plain "Plug."
Those many years had his village fame
Published the shame of his old-time game,
Till all the folks by custom came
  To call him "Plug."

And so many years at last went by
They hardly knew the reason why;
At least they never stopped to think,
And dropped the old suggestive wink.
And he took the name quite matter-of-fact,
Till most of the folks had forgot his act;
But sometimes a stranger'd wonder at
The why of a nickname such as that,
  — Of "Plug" — just "Plug."
Then some old chap would shift his quid
And tell the story of what he did.

" He owned ten acres of punkin pine,
'Twas straight and tall, and there warn't a sign
But what 'twas sound as a hickory nut,
And at last he got the price he sut.
They hired him for to chop it down.
He did. — By gosh, it was all unsoun'.
Was a rotten heart in every tree.
But there warn't none there but him to see.

And quick as ever a tree was cut,
He hewed a saplin' and plugged the butt.
— Plugged the butt, sir, and hid away
For about two months, for he'd got his pay.
But there warn't no legal actions took,
They never tackled his pocket-book.
'Twould a-broke his heart, for he's dretful snug;
But he never squirmed when they called him
  ' Plug.'
And over the whole of the country-side,
Up to the day that the critter died,
     'Twas ' Plug.'
Till some of the young folks scurcely knew
Which was the nickname, which was the true.
He left five thousand, — putty rich, —
But better less cash than a title sich
     As ' Plug.' "

THE SONG OF THE HARROW AND PLOW

From the acres of Aroostook, broad and mellow
   in the sun,
Down to rocky York, the chorus of the farmers
   has begun.
They are riding in Aroostook on a patent sulky
   plow,
— They are riding, taking comfort, for they've
   learned the secret how.
They are planting their potatoes with a whirring
   new machine,
— Driver sits beneath an awning; slickest thing
   you've ever seen.
There is not a rock to vex 'em in the acres
   spreading wide,
So they sit upon a cushion, cock their legs, and
   smoke and ride.
Gee and Bright go lurching onward in the
   furrow's mellow steam;
Over there, with clank of whiffle, tugs a sturdy
   Morgan team.
And the man who rides the planter or who plods
   the broken earth
Joins and swells the mighty chorus of the
      season's budding mirth.
   And they've pitched the tune to a jubilant
      strain.

They are lilting it merrily now.
We wait for that melody up here in Maine,
— 'Tis the song of the harrow and plow.

They are picking rocks in Oxford, and in Waldo
blasting ledge,
And they're farming down in Lincoln on their
acres set on edge.
Down among the kitchen gardens of the slopes
of Cumberland
They're sticking in the garden sass as thick as
it will stand.
And every nose is sniffing at the scent of fur-
rowed earth,
And every man is living all of life at what it's
worth.
Though the farmer in Aroostook sails across a
velvet field,
And his mellow, crumbly acres vomit forth a
spendthrift yield,
All the rest are just as cheerful on their hillside
farms as he,
For there's cosy wealth in gardens and a fortune
in a tree.
So they're singing the song of the coming
of Spring,
And the song of the empty mow;
Of the quiver of birth that is stirring the earth,
— 'Tis the song of the harrow and plow.

"There's a dretful cheery feelin' when a day's work's done."

HOORAY FOR THE SEASON OF FAIRS

This is the season for fairs, by gosh, oh, this is
    the season for fairs ;
  They're thicker than spatter,
  But what does it matter?
They scoop up the cash, but who cares?

From now till October they'll swallow the
    change,
These state fairs and town fairs and county and
    grange,
But apples blush brighter arrayed on a plate,
And the cattle look scrumptious in dignified
    state,
Enthroned in a stall and a-gazing with scorn
On the chaps going by without ribbon or horn.
And the trotters and nags of the blood-royal
    strain
Are a-furnishing fun for the people of Maine ;
While prouder than princes they prance to the
    band,
And ogle the ladies arrayed on the stand.
Ah, every exhibit in stall or in hall,
From hooked rug to hossflesh and punkin and
    all,
Takes on a new meaning, assumes a new light,
And is, for the moment, a wonderful sight.

And people hang over the stuff that's displayed,
They swig up whole barrels of red lemonade,
And hark to the fakirs and tumble to snides,
And treat all the young ones to merry-go rides.
They sit on the grand stand, man crushed
    against man,
All shouting acclaim to the track's rataplan;
And all the delight is as fresh and as bright
As though the big crowd had not seen that same
    sight.
And the people flock home with the dust in their
    eyes,
But with hearts all a-fire with fun and surprise.
The girls are a-humming the tune of the band,
And dads are relating the sights from the stand;
The dames are discussing the fancy work part,
While bub hugs the Midway scenes close to his
    heart.
The palms of the men folks still glow from a
    grip,
And the women are thinking of lip pressed to
    lip,
For all of the folks in the loud, happy throng
Have met with the friends "they've not seen
    for so long."
A hail and salute from the press of the mass,
Too brief, as the crowd jammed impatient to
    pass,

A moment — that's all — to renew the old tie,
A handgrasp, a lip-touch, " Hello," and " Good-
  by."

Oh, this is the season of fairs, by gosh, the
      season to lay off your cares,
    Each fair is a wonder,
    They're thicker than thunder.
Hooray for the season of fairs !

HAD A SET OF DOUBLE TEETH

Oh, listen while I tell to you a truthful little
   tale
  Of a man whose teeth was double all the solid
    way around;
He could jest as slick as preachin' bite in two a
   shingle nail,
  Or squonch a moulded bullet, sah, and ev'ry
    tooth was sound.

I've seen him lift a kag of pork, a-bitin' on the
   chine,
  And he'd clench a rope and hang there like a
    puppy to a root;
And a feller he could pull and twitch and yank
   upon the line,
  But he couldn't do no bus'ness with tha
    double-toothed galoot.

He was luggin' up some shingles, — bunch, sah,
   underneath each arm, —
  The time that he was shinglin' of the Baptist
    meetin'-house;
The ladder cracked and buckled, but he didn't
   think no harm,
  When all at once she busted and he started
    down kersouse.

His head, sah, when she busted, it was jest
  abreast the eaves ;
  And he nipped, sah, quicker'n lightnin', and
  he gripped there with his teeth,
And he never dropped the shingles, but he hung
  to both the sheaves,
  Though the solid ground was suttinly more'n
  thirty feet beneath.

He held there and he kicked there and he
  squirmed, but no one come.
  He was workin' on the roof alone — there
  warn't no folks around.
He hung like death to niggers till his jaws was
  set and numb,
  And he reely thought he'd have to drop them
  shingles on the ground.

But all at once old Skillins come a-toddlin' down
  the street.
  Old Skil is sort of hump-backed and he allus
  looks straight down ;
So he never see'd the motions of them Number
  'Leven feet,
  And he went a-amblin' by him — the goramded
  blind old clown !

Now this ere part is truthful — ain't a-stretchin'
    it a mite,—
  When the feller see'd that Skillins was a-
    walkin' past the place,
Let go his teeth and hollered, but he grabbed
    back quick and tight,
  'Fore he had a chance to tumble, and he hung
    there by the face.

And he never dropped the shingles and he never
    missed his grip,
  And he stepped out on the ladder when they
    raised it underneath.
And up he went a-flukin' with them shingles on
    his hip,
  — And there's the satisfaction of a havin'
    double teeth.

GRAMPY'S LULLABY

Your marmy's mixin' cream o' tartar biskit up
    for tea;
    Fie, deedle, deedle, leetle ba-a-arby!
And I reckon you had better come and roost
    upon my knee;
    Tumpy, dumpy, deedle, leetle barby!

I s'picion how ye never heard of Ebernezer
    Cowles.
Tell ye what, he warn't brung up to be afraid of
    owls.
Reckon that a spryer critter never tallered
    boots;
Allus up to monkey tricks and full o' squirms
    and scoots.
Once he done a curis thing, I yummy, on a
    stump:
Set a larder up one end and gin' a mighty jump;
Run right up the larder, jest as nimble as a
    monkey,
Balarnced, I sh'd suttin say, a minit — all a-
    hunky;
Then he straddled out on air and grabbed the
    pesky larder
And run 'er up another length — another length,
    suh, farder;

Skittered up that larder 'fore she had a chance
to teeter,
Quicker'n any pussy cat — lighter'n a mos-
keeter.
Soon's he clambered to the top, grabbed the
upper rung,
Ketched hisself with t'other hand, and there the
critter hung.
Gaffled up his britches' slack and took a resky
charnce
And thar' he held hisself right out, arms-length,
suh, by his parnts.
Ye ought ter heerd, my barby dear, the cheerins
and the howls
The crowd let out when they'd obsarved that
trick of Mister Cowles.

Sing'lar thing of which I sing — might not
think 'twas true;
    Fie, deedle, deedle, leetle ba-a-arby !
But ye know, my leetle snoozer, grampy wouldn't
lie to you,
    — To his dumpy, dumpy deedle, leetle
barby.

Hush, I guess that mammy isn't done a-makin'
bread,
We ain't at all pertic'lar how she overhears
what's said.

Ye're over-young, purraps, to hear of Sam'wel
  Doubl'yer Strout,
— Weighed about two hundred pounds, and,
  chowder, warn't he stout!
Used to work for me one time as sort of extry
  hand,
— Allus planned to 'gage him when I cleared up
  any land;
Once I see him lug a rock with fairly mod'rit
  ease
So hefty that at ev'ry step he sunk above his
  knees.
Hain't at all surprised to see the wonder in your
     eye;
    Fie, deedle, deedle, leetle ba-a-arby!
But ye know your poor old grampy wouldn't
    tell ye ary lie,
    — To his tumpy, dumpy deedle, leetle
    barby.

Course ye've never heerd 'em tell of Atha-ni-al
  Prime,
For he was round a-raisin' Cain so long afore
  your time.
Used to run the muley saw down to Hopkins
  mill,
— Allus cuttin' ding-does up — a master curis
  pill!

Once the chaps that tended sluice stood upon a
　log,
Got to argyin' this and that, suthin' 'bout a dog.
Clean forgot to start the log a-goin' up the
　sluice,
But shook their fists and hollered round and spit
　torbarker juice.
Atha-ni-al heerd the towse and grabbed a pick-
　pole up,
— Wasn't goin' to stop a mill to fight about a
　pup, —
Tied a rope around the pole and then he let her
　flam,
Speared the end of that air log and yanked her
　quicker'n Sam.
Log, suh, come right out the bark, he twitched
　the thing so quick;
Fellers never felt the yank, 'twas done so smooth
　and slick.
Log come out and up the sluice and left behind
　the bark,
— Fellers thought the log was there and stood
　and chawed till dark.
Sing'lar things has come to pass when I was
　　young as you;
　Fie, deedle, deedle, leetle ba-a-arby!
And best of all, what grampy sings you bet your
　　life is true,
　Tumpy, deedle, dumpy, leetle barby.

HOSKINS'S COW

Hoskins's cow got into the pound and the notice
   was tacked on the meetin'-house door:
" Come into my yard, one brindle cow with three
   white feet, and her shoulders sore,
— Galled by a poke, — and the owner is asked
   to call at the pound and take her away."
Well, Hoskins knew she was his all right, but,
   you see, he hadn't wherewith to pay.

The cow was breachy — she wasn't to blame,
   for Hoskins had turned her abroad to roam;
She had to battle for daily grass, for the bovine
   cupboard was bare at home.
So Hoskins had hitched on her withered neck a
   wooden "regalia" — sort of a yoke,
Supposed to keep her from breachy tricks, but
   the poor old creature employed the " poke "
To rip up fences and let down bars ; her hunger
   sharpened her slender wits,
And somehow she sneaked through the guarded
   gates, and gave the garden sass regular fits.

The neighbors pitied her starving state, but at
   last she stubbornly wouldn't shoo ;
They pounded tattoos on her skinny ribs till it
   really seemed they would whack 'em through.

But she got so toughened and callous and hard,
    and the stiffened frame of her mortised bones
Formed such an excellent armor-plate against
    the broadsides of sticks and stones,
That they "pounded" her then in a different
    way — in the village pound — whose walls
    would hold
The breachiest cow that ever strayed — and the
    notice was posted as I have told.

She stood there a day and she stayed there a
    night; she cropped the scanty bushes and
    grass,
And moo-ed and loo-ed in a yearning way, when-
    ever a person chanced to pass.
— She ate the leaves from some alder sprouts
    for a scanty breakfast the second day,
And munched the twigs for her dinner, alas,
    and longed, oh, so much, for some meadow
    hay.
That night she gnawed at her dry old poke, —
    a painful meal, for the slivers ran
In her tongue; so she crouched by the high-
    barred gate and seemed deserted of God and
    man.

And Hoskins knew that they had his cow and
    Hoskins knew of her solemn fast.

For he'd gone up the highway and looked
through the gate in her dumb, reproachful eyes
as he passed.
Yet what, may I ask, could the poor man do?
He was right in a place where he couldn't
pay,
— He had three dollars, 'tis true enough, and
'twould square the bill, but, you see, that day
The catchers had come and taken his dogs: a
hound, a setter, and brindle-pup,
And a man like Hoskins would ne'er endure to
have the dog-pound gobble them up,
For he gunned on Sundays behind the hound,
and the bull was entered and backed to fight.
And Hoskins, you see, as a sporting man had a
reputation to keep upright.
I wonder, friends, if you've ever thought, while
you've stormed at rum as the poor man's curse,
There are chaps so built on the mental plan that
keeping dogs will warp them worse?
The "two-dog" man may be reclaimed, but I've
been compelled, alas, to see
That there doesn't appear to be much hope for
the wretched critter condemned to three.
And Hoskins's duty was plain to him: his
youngsters wailed for the milk they missed,
But Hoskins thought of his poor, poor dogs and
gripped his dollars tight in his fist.

He shut his ears to his children's cries, he steeled
    his heart when he passed the pound,
To the mute appeal in the old cow's eyes; but
    he smiled at last when his dogs were found.
And he gladly proffered the three lone plunks
    to sate the greed of the legal hogs,
And proudly he took the highway back, a-lead-
    ing his licensed, bailed-out dogs.
And they barked and yipped and yapped and
    yawped at a poor old tottering cow they found
Absorbed in a desperate, hungry reach for a
    thistle outside the village pound.

AN OLD STUN' WALL

If ye only knew the backaches in an old stun'
wall!
   O, Lordy me,
   I'm seventy-three!
— Begun amongst these boulders and I've lived
here through it all.
I wasn't quite to bub's age there, when dad
commenced to clear
The wust of ninety acres with a hoss team and
a steer.
And we've used the stun's for fencin' and we've
built around the lot,
O, I've tugged and worked there, sonny, ontil
gracious me, I've sot
And fairly groaned o' evenings with the twinges
in my back;
Sakes, there warn't no shirkin,' them days; it
was tug and lift and sack,
For it needed lots of muscle, lots of gruntin',
lots of sand
If a feller calculated for to clear a piece of
land.
Bub, it isn't any wonder that our backs has got
a hump,
That our arms are stretched and awkward like
the handle on a pump,

That our palms are hard and calloused, that we
    wobble in our gait
— There's the reason right before you 'round
    the medders in the State.
And I wonder sometimes, sonny, that we've
    any backs at all
When I figer on the backaches in an
                  Old
                      Stun'
                          Wall.
If ye only knew the backaches in an old stun'
    wall!
      We read of men
      Who with a pen
Have pried away the curses that have crushed
    us in their fall.
I don't begrudge them honor nor the splendor
    of their name
For an av'rage Yankee farmer hasn't any use
    for fame,
But the man who lifted curses and the man
    who lifted stones
Never'll hear a mite of diff'runce in the
    Heavenly Father's tones.
For I have the humble notion, bub, that when
    all kinds of men,
The chaps that pried with crowbar and the
    chaps that pried with pen,

Are waitin' to be measured for the things
   they've done below
The angel with the girth-chain's bound to give
   us all fair show.
And the humble man who's tussled with the
   rocks of stubborn Maine
Won't find that all his labor has been thankless
   and in vain.
And while the wise and mighty get the glorious
   credit due
The man who took the brunt of toil will be
   remembered too.
The man who bent his aching back will earn
   his crown, my child,
By the acres he made fertile and the miles of
   rocks he piled.
That ain't my whole religion, for I don't propose
   to shirk
What my duties are to Heaven,— but the gospel
   of hard work
Is a mighty solid bed-rock that I've built on
   more or less ;
I believe that God Almighty has it in his heart
   to bless
For the good they've left behind them rough old
   chaps with humped-up backs
Who have gone ahead and smoothed things with
   the crowbar and the axe.

For if all our hairs are numbered and He notes
   the sparrow's fall
He understands the backaches in an
                        Old
                              Stun'
                                    Wall.

THE STOCK IN THE TIE-UP

I'm workin' this week in the wood lot; a hearty
    old job, you can bet;
I finish my chores with a larntern, and marm has
    the table all set
By the time I get in with the milkin'; and after
    I wash at the sink,
And marm sets a saucer o' strainin's for the cat
    and the kittens to drink,
Your uncle is ready for supper, with an appetite
    whet to an edge
That'll cut like a bush-scythe in swale-grass, and
    couldn't be dulled on a ledge.
And marm, she slats open the oven, and pulls
    out a heapin' full tin
Of the rippin'est cream-tartar biskit a man ever
    pushed at his chin.
We pile some more wood on the fire, and open
    the damper full blare,
And pull up and pitch into supper — and com-
    fort — and taste good — wal, there!
And the wind swooshes over the chimbly, and
    scrapes at the shingles cross grain,
But good double winders and bankin' are mighty
    good friends here in Maine.
I look 'crost the table to mother, and marm she
    looks over at me,

And passes another hot biskit and says, " Won't
ye have some more tea? "
And while I am stirrin' the sugar, I relish the
sound of the storm.
For, thank the good Lord, we are cosy and the
stock in the tie-up is warm.

I tell ye, the song o' the fire and the chirruping
hiss o' the tea,
The roar of the wind in the chimbly, they sound
dreadful cheerful to me.
But they'd harrer me, plague me, and fret me,
unless as I set here I knew
That the critters are munchin' their fodder and
bedded and comf'table too.
These biskits are light as a feather, but, boy,
they'd be heavier'n lead
If I thought that my hosses was shiv'rin', if I
thought that my cattle warn't fed.
There's men in the neighborhood 'round me who
pray som'w'at louder than me,
They wear better clothes, sir, on Sunday — chip
in for the heathen Chinee,
But the cracks in the sides o' their tie-ups are
wide as the door o' their pew,
And the winter comes in there a-howlin', with
the sleet and the snow peltin' through.

Step in there, sir, ary a mornin' and look at their
  critters ! 'Twould seem
As if they were bilers or engines, and all o'
  them chock full o' steam.
I've got an old-fashioned religion that calkalates
  Sundays for rest,
But if there warn't time, sir, on week days to
  batten a tie-up, I'm blest
I'd use up a Sunday or such-like, and let the
  durned heathen folks go
While I fastened some boards on the lintel to
  keep out the frost and the snow.
I'd stand all the frowns of the parson before I'd
  have courage to face
The dumb holler eyes o' the critters hooked up
  in a frosty old place.
And I'll bet ye that in the Hereafter the men
  who have stayed on their knees
And let some poor, fuzzy old cattle stand out in
  a tie-up and freeze,
Will find that the heat o' the Hot Place is keyed
  to an extra degree
For the men who forgot to consider that critters
  have feelin's same's we.

I dasn't go thinkin' o' tie-ups where winter goes
  whistlin' through.
Where cattle are humped at their stanchions
  with scarcely the gumption to moo.

But I'm glad for the sake of Hereafter that
  mine ain't the sin and the guilt,
And I tell you I relish my feelin's when I pull
  up the big patchwork quilt.
I can laugh at the pelt o' the snowflakes, and
  grin at the slat o' the storm,
And thank the good Lord I can sleep now; the
  stock in the tie-up is warm.

EPHRUM WADE'S STAND–BY IN HAYING

Ephrum Wade sat down in the shade
And took off his haymaker hat, which he laid
On a tussock of grass; and he pulled out the
    plug
That jealously gagged the old iron-stone jug.
And cocking his jug on his elbow he rigged
A sort of a "horse-up," you know, and he
    swigged
A pint of hard cider or so at a crack,
And set down the jug with a satisfied smack.
"Aha!" said he, "that grows the hair on ye,
    bub,
My rule durin' hayin's more cider, less grub.
I take it, sah, wholly to stiddy my nerves,
And up in the stow hole I pitch 'em some
    curves
On a drink of straight cider, in harnsomer shape
Than a feller could do on the juice of the grape.
Some new folderinos come 'long every day,
All sorts of new jiggers to help git yer hay.
Improvements on cutter bars, hoss forks, and
    rakes,
And tedders and spreaders and all of them fakes.
But all of their patents ain't fixed it so yit
That hayin' is done without git-up and git.

If ye want the right stuff, sah, to take up the
    slack,
The stuff to put buckram right inter yer back,
The stuff that will limber and ile up yer j'ints,
Just trot out some cider and drink it by pints.
It ain't got no patents — it helps you make hay
As it helped out our dads in their old-fashioned
    way.
Molasses and ginger and water won't do,
'Twill irrigate some, but it won't see ye through.
And ice water 'll chill ye, and skim milk is durn
Mean stuff any place, sah, except in a churn.
I'm a temperate man as a general rule,
—The man who gits bit by the adder's a fool, —
But when it comes hayin' and folks have to strain,
I tell you, old cider's a stand-by in Maine."

Then Ephrum Wade reclined in the shade
And patiently gazed on the hay while it " made."

RESURRECTION OF EPHRUM WAY

Old Uncle Ephrum Isaac Way
— He had a fit the other day.
A sort of capuluptic spell;
He hasn't been in no ways well
Since year ago come next July;
He had a sunstroke; come blamed nigh
To passin' 'crost. And since, for him,
The poor old man's been dretful slim.
And 'twarn't surprisin' none, I say,
That fit of his the other day.
By time that Dr. Blaisdell come
His legs and arms had growed all numb.
He didn't sense things scurce at all,
His lower jaw commenced to fall,
And, jedged from looks, there warn't no doubt
That Ephrum's soul was passin' out.
Fact is, they thought that he was dead;
They tied the bandage round his head,
Laid out his shroud — when first they knew,
Eph kicked awhile and then come to;
Got up and stared with all his eyes,
And said, " Why, this ain't Paradise!
Gol durn the luck, they let me in;
Now here I'm back on earth agin.
I've been to Heaven! I've been dead,
I've seen it All," so Ephrum said.

And while we gathered round with awe
He told us all the things he saw.
And while he yarned that tale of Death
The parson came, all out of breath,
Exclaiming o'er and o'er again,
"A vision! Wondrous! Blest of men!"
And asked, "Oh, tell us, Mr. Way,
How long were you allowed to stay?"
And then the crowd hung breathless round
A-harkin' until Ephrum found
Some sort of language in his reach,
— For he was sort of dull in speech.
" Wal, friends," he slowly said at last,
"I ricollect that when I passed
The pearly gates and sills of gold
And see that blessed sight unfold
Before my dim old hazy eyes,
I got a shock of such surprise
I couldn't move, — I couldn't speak,
— Jest run my tongue down in my cheek
And sort of numbly pronged and pried
The chaw I took before I died.
— That's been my habit all my days;
When I am nervous anyways
I don't fly all to gosh.   Instid
I simply, calmly shift my quid.
But jest as I had rolled her 'crost —
Wal, suthin' dropped and I was lost.

And all of Heaven, friends, I saw
Was while I shifted that air chaw."
I think, dear sir, I scarce need add
That seldom do you see so glad
A resurrection time as they
Who stood there gave old Ephrum Way.
The parson first he tried to screw
His face up solemn, but that crew
Broke out and howled like they was daft.
And so he laughed and laughed and laughed.

LOOK OUT FOR YOUR THUMB

Hindsight is clearer than foresight,
  But foresight is better and safer, old chap.
Experiment teaches, but common sense reaches
  And tests the bright baubles in Dame Future's
    lap.

I'm telling you what Eph Landers did
The time that the critter lost his fid.

He was sort of a quick, impulsive man;
— When others walked, he always ran.

He never waited to calmly view,
But he got right up and slam-banged through.

Believed that the moments a feller took
To give the future a good square look

Was simply so much wasted time;
His plan was, " Never look up; just climb."

He was yankin' boulders a week ago
And things got balky and movin' slow.

He strung the chain 'round a good big rock
And found that he'd lost the little block

To catch the link; it's used instid
Of a hook and link, and it's called a fid.

And Eph, he held the unhooked chain
By the ends, and he looked and he got profane.

But he couldn't find it and wouldn't wait,
— He was mad as a bug and desperate,

And the crack-brained critter — what do ye
 think?
Why, he stuck his thumb in the unhooked link.

He didn't consider that 'twarn't his fid,
But the oxen started — and then he did!

He see'd his mistake, as most men do,
When the deed is done and the thing is through:

You stick your thumb where it don't belong
And the world will yank it, good and strong.

Hindsight is clearer than foresight,
 But you'd better ask foresight to give ye a
  point ;
Or, first thing you're knowin', Old World will be
  goin',
And he'll laugh while you howl with your thumb
  out of joint.

THE TRIUMPH OF MODEST MARIA

Maria's comb hung lopsy-wise
And flapped athwart her filmy eyes,
Exactly like a slattern's hair
On washing day; and I declare
She was the slouchiest-looking hen
That pecked in T. B. Tucker's pen.
    Cah-dah! Cah-dut!
    She was the butt
Of every sort of jibe and cut.

Maria was a Brahma dame,
Broad and squat and plucked and lame.
The Leghorns cast a pitying smile
Upon her queer, old-fashioned style.
The Plymouth Rocks would jeer and flout
Because her legs were feathered out.
    The cocks would strut,
    Pah-rutt! Pah-rutt!
And snigger at her bloomers' cut.

The trim white Cochins tip-toed by
And froze her with disdainful eye;
Each tufted Houdan tossed her plume
And glared Maria's social doom.
Where'er she strolled in all the yard
Maria got it good and hard!

Cah-dut! Cah-dah!
Each social star
Just dropped Maria with a jar.

But she pursued her quiet way,
And picked and scratched the livelong day,
Kept early hours and ate bran mash,
Nor sought to cut a social dash.
And then one day she left her nest
With pallid comb and swelling breast.
Cah-dut! Cah-dah!
Hooray, hurrah!
Maria, you're a queen, you are!

The news went cackling round the pen
— An egg! It measured twelve by ten.
And T. B. Tucker drove to town
To take that gor-rammed big egg down.
The editor put on his specs,
The villagers turned rubber necks,
And some collecting feller paid
Right smart for what Maria laid.
And European news was set
Aside that week by the *Gazette*
In order that a glowing pen
Might pay due praise to that old hen.
Cah-lip! Cah-lop!
You'll find, sure pop,
That modest merit lands on top.

SON HAS GOT THE DEED

Mother fights with Marshy, and Marshy fights
  with her,
— Don't give up yer proputty, I'm tellin' on yer,
  sir!
Don't give up yer proputty to nary blessed one,
— Don't keer whuther brother, sir, or nephy,
  sir, or son.
Don't make over northin', sir, ontil you're done
  and through,
Or ye'll cuss the day ye done it till the air is
  black and blue.
Me and marm got feeble and we couldn't run
  the farm,
Son was newly married and we couldn't see the
  harm
In makin' on it over, we to have the ell and shed,
Use the sittin' room in common — and a room
  for one spare bed.
And so we made the papers and we signed 'em,
  me and wife,
'Lowin' them the stand and stock, and us our
  keep for life.
Twelvemonth isn't finished, but the trouble has
  begun,
An' it's one continyal rowin' 'twixt us and her
  and son.

Marshy dings at mother and mother dings at her,
'F things ain't settled somehow, sir, they'll git
   to clawin' fur.

Don't give up yer proputty, I'm tellin' on ye
   straight.
Don't keer who your family is, ye'll rue it sure
   as fate.
'Fore ye sign the papers they'll come round ye
   slicker'n cream,
But ye'll notice little later, sir, that things ain't
   what they seem.
Man that's got his proputty, he's looked to with
   respect ;
Relations they come meechin' round to
   scratch, sir, where he's pecked.
Ye see, he rules the family roost and leads the
   family flock,
As proud and full of manners as a Cochin China
   cock.
But if the years have loosened up his intellect
   and grip,
And if he thinks his folks are straight, and lets
   the old farm slip,
He'll find the grin becomes a frown and sweetness turns to greed,
For folks see things in different light when once
   they've got a deed.

Now Marshy snarls at mother and mother sends
   it back,
And all the time, from sun to sun, it's clack and
   clack and clack!

Don't give up yer propputy, hang on till death,
   I say;
It's time when you are done with it to give your
   all away.
Oh, how the devil snickers round when some
   old codger drools
About "the laying down of cares" — and jines
   the ranks of fools!
And how the lawyers laugh and joke, and how
   the angels weep,
To see some old folks deed away their farm for
   board and keep!
— Never see'd no better cook than Marshy
   used to be,
When first along she'd ask us down to dinner
   or to tea.
Used to sweeten grub with smiles when she
   would pass a plate,
And me and marm, like two old coots, we swallowed hook and bait.
You bet we git some diff'rent looks, we git some
   diff'rent feed,

Jest like they'd throw it out to dogs, now son
    has got the deed.
An' Marshy growls at mother, and mother's
    growlin' wuss,
An' I — wal, I jest set and smoke and cuss —
    and cuss — and cuss!

AN IDYL OF COLD WEATHER

When all the sky seems blazing down, and sun-
shine curls the bricks,
And General Humidity puts in his biggest licks,
I welcome to my eyry, with a moist and dripping
palm,
A placid old philosopher who runs a little farm,
Who says imagination helps a deal in keeping
cool,
And who to comfort other men makes this his
simple rule:
To talk of piping, biting days, and drifting
winter storm
Whene'er the weather pipes it up and gets too
thunderin' warm.
They're better far than fizz or smash or juleps,
sure's you're born,
— The honest little narratives of Frigid Weather
John.
For though the sizzling summer time may boil
and steam and hiss,
Who'd ever, ever think of it while listening to
this?

" I never see'd a winter have a durnder, sharper
aidge
Than in the year of Sixty-one, the year that I
drove stage.

I never had so hard a job attendin' to my biz,
For everything 't was frizable, that year you bet
   was friz.
At last I done a caper that I hadn't done for
   years :
I got a little careless and I friz up both my ears.
The roads was awful drifted and I trod ten
   miles of snow,
And all the time that zippin' wind did nothin',
   sah, but blow.
Them ears of mine was froze so hard, stuck out
   so bloomin' straight,
I thought the wind would snap 'em off, it blew
   at such a rate.
And when at last I hauled up home, the missus
   bust in tears
And hollered, ' John, oh, massy me, you're going
   to lose your ears.'
But I — why, land o' goodness, I was cooler'n I
   be now,"
— And he passed his red bandanna up across
   his steaming brow,—
"I jest got out my hatchet and I chopped two
   cakes of ice
And held 'em on my friz-up ears — 'twas
   Granpy Jones' advice.
I didn't dast go in the house, but set there in
   the shed

A-holdin' them two chunks of ice to either
    side my head.
The chunks weighed fifty pounds apiece — that
    doctorin' didn't cost —
And so I got 'em big enough to take out all the
    frost.
My wife came out at last to see what made me
    keep so still,
And there I was, sah, sound asleep and snorin'
    fit to kill.
She got me in and gave me tea and helped me
    inter bed,
With that 'ere ice a-frozen tight and solid to my
    head.
'Twas sort of curi's, I confess, but still I slept
    complete,
A crystal palace on my head and soapstones on
    my feet.
It wasn't really what you'd call a calm and rest-
    ful night,
But when the ice peeled off next day them ears
    come out all right."

They're better far than fizz or smash or juleps,
    sure's you're born,
— These honest little narratives from Frigid
    Weather John.

BUSTED THE "TEST YOUR STRENGTH"

When pa was down to Topsham fair
I snooped around and heard him swear
To Jotham Briggs that it seemed to him
That muscle nowadays was slim,
For he said he'd stood there quite a length,
Seein' folks whang at the " test your strength,"
And there wasn't a one in all that spell
Who'd hit a crack that had tapped the bell.
And pa talked loud and he sassed the crowd,
And the crowd sassed pa, and he allowed
He'd show 'em what; and so old Jote
Just held his hat and his vest and coat;
And pa he rolled his sleeves up tight,
Hauled out his plug and took a bite.
He whirled one arm in wind-mill style,
— Then whirled the other one awhile.
He picked his pessle out at length
And sassed the great, tall " test your strength."
" I'm goin' to soak ye now," says pa,
" You'll think it's y'earthquakes by the jar.
Git out the way and giv' me swing,
— I'll bust the ha'slet out the thing."
And pa he spit in both his fists
And give the handle two three twists,
And swung the beetle round and round
To give one big, gol-rippin' pound.

One knee was right up 'ginst his chin,
His eyes stuck out, his lips sucked in,
And down he fetched her with a jolt,
But pa — but pa — he missed his holt!
He lost his grip, the pessle flew,
And folks they scattered, I tell you.
Some chaps fell down and some they ducked,
And them fur off, by gosh, they hucked.
For that air pessle, sir, it come
Sky-hootin' like a ten-inch bumb.
It landed more'n eight rods away
Right through the top of Drew's new shay,
— Right 'twixt the gal and Ezry Drew,
And hully gee, it scart 'em blue.
While pa — wal, pa, he jest turned green
— Gawked fust at Drew, then that machine.
And hammed and stuttered out at length,
" I aimed 'er at that ' test your strength ' ! "
" Good eye ! " says Ez, as mad as sin,
And then he snorted, " Drunk agin ! "
And pa — wal, warn't a thing to say,
'Cept pull, — and ask Ez, " What's to pay ? "

"WHEN A MAN GETS OLD"

The clash and the clatter of mowing-machines
Float up where the old man stands and leans
His trembling hands on the worn old snath,
As he looks afar in the broadening path,
Where the shivering grasses melt beneath
A seven-foot bar and its chattering teeth.

When a man gits old, says he,
    When a man gits old,
He is mighty small pettaters
    As I've just been told.
I used to mow at the head of the crew,
And I cut a swath that was wide as two.
— Covered a yard, sah, at every sweep;
The man that follered me had to leap.
I made the best of the critters squeal,
And nary a feller could nick my heel.
The crowd that follered, they took my road
As I walked away from the best that mowed.
But I can't keep up with the boys no more,
My arms are stiff and my cords are sore:
And they've given this rusty scythe to me
— It has hung two years in an apple-tree —
And told me to trim along the edge
Where the mowing-machine has skipped the
    ledge.

It seems, sah, skurcely a year ago
That I was a-showin' 'em how to mow,
A-showin' 'em how, with the tanglin' grass
Topplin' and fallin', to let me pass ;
A-showing 'em how, with a five-foot steel,
And never a man who could nick my heel.
But now it's the day of the hot young blood,
And I'm doin' the job of the fuddy-dud ;
Hacking the sides of the dusty road
And the corner clumps where the men ain't
    mowed.
And that's the way, a man gits told,
He's smaller pettaters when he grows old.

I'VE GOT THEM CALVES TO VEAL

It's a jolly sort of season, is the spring — is the spring,
And there isn't any reason for not feeling like a king.
The sun has got flirtatious and he kisses Mistress Maine,
And she pouts her lips, a-saying, " Mister, can't you come again ? "
The hens are all a-laying, the potatoes sprouting well,
And fodder spent so nicely that I'll have some hay to sell.
But when I get to feeling just as well as I can feel,
All to once it comes across me that I've got them calves to veal.

Oh ! I can't go in the stanchion, look them mothers in the eye,
For I'm meditatin' murder ; planning how their calves must die.
Every time them little shavers grab a teat, it wrings my heart,
— Hate to see 'em all so happy, for them cows and calves must part.
That's the reason I'm so mournful ; that's the reason in the spring

I go feeling just like Nero or some other wicked
 thing,
For I have to slash and slaughter; have to set
 an iron heel
On the feelings of them mothers; I have got
 them calves to veal.

Spring is happy for the poet and the lover and
 the girl,
But the farmer has to do things that will make
 his harslet curl.
And the thing that hits me hardest is to stand
 the lonesome moos
Of that stanchion full of critters when they find
 they're going to lose
Little Spark-face, Little Brindle — when the
 time has come to part,
And the calves go off a-blatting in a butcher's
 rattling cart.
Though the cash the butcher pays me sort of
 smooths things up and salves
All the really rawest feeling when I sell them
 little calves,
Still I'm mournful in the springtime; knocks
 me off my even keel,
Seeing suffering around me when I have them
 calves to veal.

THE OFF SIDE OF THE COW

Old Wendell Hopkins' hired man is an absent-
minded chap,
He'll start for a chair, and like as not set down
in some one's lap.
I happened along where he stopped to bait his
hosses the other day,
— He'd given the hosses his luncheon pail and
was trying to eat their hay,
— A kind of a blame fool sort of a trick for even
a hired man,
But he tackled a different kind of a snag when
he fooled with Matilda Ann,
— When he fooled with Matilda Ann, by jinks,
he got it square in the neck,
And the doctors say, though live he may, he's a
total human wreck.
    He's wrapped in batting and thinking now
    Of the grief in insulting a brindle cow.

Matilda Ann gives down her milk and she
doesn't switch her tail;
She gives ten quarts — week in, week out, and
she never kicks the pail.
She doesn't hook and she doesn't jump, but even
Matilda Ann
Ain't called to stand all sorts of grief from a
dern fool hired man.

And when he stubbed to the milking-shed in
    sort of a dream and tried
To make Matilda "So" and "Whoa" while he
    milked on the wrong, off side,
She giv' him a look to wilt his soul and pugged
    him once with her hoof,
And I guess that at last his wits were jogged as
    he slammed through the lintel roof.
       He's got a poultice on his brow
       Of the size of the foot of a brindle cow.

Now study the ways of the world, my son ; oh,
    study the ways of life !
It's the hustling chap that gets the cash, or the
    girl he wants for a wife ;
It's the feller that spots the place to grab, when
    Chance goes swinging by,
Who gets his dab in the juiciest place and the
    biggest plum in the pie ;
There's always a chance to milk the world —
    there's a teat, a pail, and a stool ;
There's a place for the chap with sense and grip,
    but a dangerous holt for a fool.
For while the feller that's up to snuff drums a
    merry tune in his pail,
The fool sneaks up on the left-hand side and
    lands in the grave or in jail.
       — It's an awkard place, as you'll allow,
       The off-hand side of the world or a cow.

THE LYRIC OF THE BUCK-SAW

Ur-r rick, ur-r raw,
Ur-r rick, ur-r raw!
Have you buckled your back to an old buck-saw?
Have you doubled your knee on a knotty stick
And bobbed to the tune of ur-r raw, ur-r rick?
Have you sawed till your eye-balls goggled and
    popped,
Till your heart seemed lead and your breath was
    stopped?
Have you yeaked her up and yawked her down,
— As doleful a lad as there was in town?
If so, we can talk of the back-bent woe
That followed the youngsters of long ago.
Ah, urban chap, with your anthracite,
Pass on, for you cannot fathom, quite,
The talk that I make with this other chap
Who got no cuddling in Comfort's lap.
You'll scarcely follow me when I sing
Of the rasping buck-saw's dancing spring,
For the rugged rhythm is fashioned for
The ear that remembers ur-r rick, ur-r raw.

Ur-r raw, ur-r rick.
Ur-r raw, ur-r rick!
We pecked at our mountain stick by stick.
Our dad was a man who was mighty good
In getting the women-folks lots of wood.

And as soon as sledding came on to stay
Jack got all work and he got no play.
For daily the ox-sleds creaked and crawked
Till the yard was full and the buck-saws talked.
'Twas rugged toil and we humped our backs,
But we scarce kept pace with dad's big axe.
There were bitter mornings of "ten below,"
There were days of bluster and days of snow,
But with double mittens, a big wool scarf,
And coon-skin ear-laps, we used to laugh
At the fussiest blast old Boreas shrieked,
And the nippingest pinches Jack Frost tweaked,
We were warm as the blade of the yanking saw
That steamed to the tune of ur-r rick, ur-r raw!

　　　　Ur–r raw, ur–r rick,
　　　　Ur–r raw, ur–r rick!
Ho, men at the desks, there, dull and sick!
You slap your hands to your stiff old backs
At thought of the days of the saw and axe;
And you press your palms to an aching brow,
And shiver to think of a saw-buck now.
But ah, old fellows, you can't deny
You hanker a bit for the times gone by,
When the toil of the tasks that filled the day
Made bright by contrast our bits of play.
Oh, grateful the hour at set of sun,
When the tea was hot, and the biscuits "done;"

When chocking his axe in the chopping-block,
Dad sung, " Knock off, boys, five o'clock."
Now tell me truly, ye wearied men,
Are you ever as happy as you were then,
When you straightened your toil-bent, weary
   backs
At the welcome plop of dad's old axe?
And tell me truly, can you forget
The sight of the table that mother set,
When dropping the saws in the twilight gloom,
We trooped to the cheer of the dear fore-room,
And there in the red shade's mellow light
Made feast with a grand good appetite?
— Made feast at the sweet old homespun board
On the plum preserves and the " crab jell " stored
For demands like these; and made great holes
In the heaps of the cream o' tartar rolls?
Ah, gusto! fickle and faint above
The savory viands you used to love,
What wouldn't you give for the sharp-set tang
That followed those days when the steel teeth
   sang?
— For zest was as keen as the bright, swift saw
When you humped to the tune of ur-r rick,
   ur-r raw?

MISTER KEAZLE'S EPITAPH

Foster the tinker traversed Maine
　　From Elkinstown to Kittery Point,
With a rattling pack and a rattling brain,
　　And a general air of " out of joint."
A gaunt old chap with a shambling gait,
　　A battered hat, and rusty clothes,
With grimy digits in sorry state,
　　And a smooch on the end of his big red nose.
　　　That was the way that Foster went,
　　　— Mixture of shrewdness and folly blent,
　　　Mending the pots and the pans as ordered,
　　　But leaving the leak in his nob unsoldered.

But Foster the tinker was no one's fool;
　　He fired an answer every time.
'Twas either a saw or proverb or rule,
　　Or else a bit of home-made rhyme.
And while he knocked at a pot or a pan
　　And puffed the coals of his little blaze,
He was ready and primed for the jocose man
　　Who thought that the tinker was easy to
　　　　phase.
　　　It chanced that Foster stopped one night
　　　With a man who thought a master sight
　　　Of being esteemed as smart's a weasel
　　　— Man by the name of Obed Keazle.

And he pronged at Foster the evening through
  While the folks were having a merry laugh;
And they laughed the most when he said, "Now
      you
  Compose me a good nice epitaph,
And your lodging here shan't cost a cent."
  So Foster snapped at the chance and said
He would have it ready before he went,
  And would make one verse ere they went to
    bed.
    So Keazle listened with deep delight
    While he heard the guileless chap recite,
    With his head a-cock like a huge canary,
    This sample of his obituary:
        Thus he begun
        Verse number one:

"A man there was who died of late,
Whom angels did impatient wait,
With outstretched arms and smiles of love
To bear him to the Realms Above."

Foster the tinker slept that night
  On a feather tick that was three feet thick,
And Keazle attended in calm delight
  To warm the bed with a nice hot brick.
And the tinker sat at the breakfast board
  And blandly smiled and ate and ate,

Then piled on his back his motley hoard
  And took his stand at the front yard gate.
    He said, " I'll give ye the other half
    Of that strictly fust-class epitaph."
    There are doubts you know as to how it
      suited,
    But the tinker didn't wait — he scooted.
        For thus ran — whew !
        Verse number two :

" While angels hovered in the skies
Disputing who should bear the prize,
In slipped the devil like a weasel
And Down Below he kicked old Keazle."

PLAIN OLD KITCHEN CHAP

Mother's furnished up the parlor — got a full,
    new haircloth set,
And there ain't a neater parlor in the county,
    now, I'll bet.
She has been a-hoarding pennies for a mighty
    tedious time ;
She has had the chicken money, and she's saved
    it, every dime.
And she's put it out in pictures and in easy
    chairs and rugs,
— Got the neighbors all a-sniffin' 'cause we're
    puttin' on such lugs.
Got up curtains round the winders, whiter'n
    snow and all of lace,
Fixed that parlor till, by gracious, I should never
    know the place.
And she says as soon's it's settled she shall give
    a yaller tea.
And invite the whole caboodle of the neighbors
    in to see.
Can't own up that I approve it; seems too much
    like fubb and fuss
To a man who's lived as I have — jest a blamed
    old kitchen cuss.

Course we've had a front room always ; tidy place
    enough, I guess,
Couldn't tell, I never set there, never opened it
    unless
Parson called, or sometimes mother give a party
    or a bee,
When the women come and quilted and the men
    dropped round to tea.
Now we're goin' to use it common. Mother
    says it's time to start,
If we're any better'n heathens, so's to sweeten
    life with art.
Says I've grubbed too long with plain things,
    haven't lifted up my soul.
Says I've denned there in the kitchen like a
    woodchuck in his hole.
— It's along with other notions mother's getting
    from the club ;
But I've got no growl a-comin', mother ain't let
    up on grub !
Still I'm wishin' she would let me have my
    smoke and take my nap
In the corner, side the woodbox ; I'm a plain old
    kitchen chap.

I have done my stent at farmin'; folks will tell
    you I'm no shirk ;
There's the callus on them fingers, that's the
    badge of honest work.

And them hours in the corner when I've stum-
    bled home to rest
Have been earnt by honest labor and they've
    been my very best.
Land! If I could have a palace wouldn't ask no
    better nook
Than this corner in the kitchen with my pipe
    and some good book.
I'm a sort of dull old codger, clear behind the
    times, I s'pose;
Stay at home and mind my bus'ness; wear some
    pretty rusty clothes;
'Druther set out here'n the kitchen, have for
    forty years or more,
Till the heel of that old rocker's gouged a holler
    in the floor;
Set my boots behind the cook stove, dry my old
    blue woolen socks,
Get my knife and plug tobacker from that dented
    old tin box,
Set and smoke and look at mother clearing up
    the things from tea;
— Rather tame for city fellers, but that's fun
    enough for me.
I am proud of mother's parlor, but I'm feared
    the thing has put
Curi's notions in her noddle, for she says I'm
    underfoot;

Thinks we oughter light the parlor, get a crowd
  and ontertain,
But I ain't no city loafer, — I'm a farmer down in
  Maine.
Course I can't hurt mother's feelin's, wouldn't
  do it for a mint,
Yet that parlor business sticks me, and I guess
  I'll have to hint
That I ain't an ontertainer, and I'll leave that
  job to son ;
I'll set out here in the kitchen while the folks
  are having fun.
And if marm comes out to get me, I will pull
  her on my lap,
And she'll know — and she'll forgive me, for I'm
  jest a kitchen chap.

TAKIN' COMFORT

I wouldn't be an emp'ror after supper's cleared
    away ;
  I wouldn't be a king, suh, if I could.
So long as I've got health and strength, a home
    where I can stay,
  And a woodshed full of dry and fitted wood.
For Jimmy brings the bootjack, and mother trims
    the light,
And pulls the roller curtains, shettin' out the
    stormy night.
And me and Jim and mother and the cat set
    down —
  Oh, who in tunket hankers for a crown?

Who wants to spend their ev'nin's sittin'
    starched and prim and straight,
  A-warmin' royal velvet on a throne ?
It's mighty tedious bus'ness settin' up so
    thund'rin' late,
  With not a minit's time to call your own.
I'd rather take my comfort after workin' through
    the days
With my old blue woolen stockin's nigh the
    fire's social blaze,
For me and Jim and mother and the old gray cat
  Come mighty near to knowin' where we're at.

EPHRUM KEPT THREE DOGS

Ephrum Eels he had to scratch durned hard to
    keep ahead,
    — But he always kept three dogs.
He couldn't keep a dollar bill to save his life,
    they said,
    — But he always kept three dogs.
He said he might have been some one if he'd
    had half a chance,
But getting grub from day to day giv' Ephrum
    such a dance,
He never got where he could shed the patches
    off his pants;
    — But he always kept three dogs.

Ephrum's young ones never looked as though
    they was half-fed,
    — But he always kept three dogs.
The house would be so cold his folks would
    have to go to bed;
    — But Ephrum kept three dogs.
One was sort of setter dog and two of 'em was
    houn's,
Their skins was full of Satan; they was always
    on their roun's,
Till people durned their pictures in half a dozen
    towns,
    — But Ephrum kept his dogs.

They 'bated Ephrum's poll-tax 'cause he was too
     poor to pay,
     — But Ephrum kept his dogs.
How he scraped up cash to license 'em it ain't
     in me to say,
     — But I know he kept his dogs.
And when a suff'rin' neighbor ambuscaded 'em,
     Eph swore —
Then in a kind of homesick way he hustled
     round for more ;
He struck a lucky bargain and, by thunder, he
     bought four !
     — Jest kept on a-keepin' dogs.

LAY OF DRIED–APPLE PIE

Sunning themselves on the southern porch,
Where the warm fall rays from the towering
    torch
Of the great sun flash in the glowing noons,
The drying apples, in long festoons,
Drink the breath of the crisp fall days,
Borrow the blush of the warming rays;
Storing their sweetness, their rich bouquet,
Against that savage and wintry day
When the housewife's fingers shall by and by
Mould them into dried-apple pie.

There they mellow and there they brown,
Homely enough to a man from town,
Merely strings of some shrunken fruit,
Swung in the sun.   And yet they're mute
Memory-ticklers to those who know
The ways of the farm in the long-ago:
— The kitchen table, the heaping store
Of round, red apples upon the floor.
The purr of the parer, the mellow snip
As the busy knives thro' the apples slip.
The merry chatter of boys and girls,
The rosy clutter of paring curls,
As hurrying knives and fingers fly
O'er the luscious fruit for dried-apple pie.

I'm idly thinking it sure must be
That the rollicking sport of the apple-bee,
— The sweetness of smiles, the touch of the
    white
Hands flashing there in the candle-light, —
Must all in a mystic way be blent
In one grand flavor; — that such was lent
To those mellowing strings, those festoons dun
Swinging there in the late fall sun.
For lo, as I look I seem to see
A dream of the past, a fantasy,
— A laughing, black-eyed roguish girl
Whirling a writhing paring curl;
Chanting the words of the old mock spell
That all we children knew so well:
" Three times round and down you go!
Now who is the one that loves me so? "

.   .   .   Merely a fancy, a passing gleam
Of the old, old days; — a sudden dream
Beguiled by some prank of a blurring eye
And the tricking song of a big, blue fly;
— Merely a fancy, and yet, ah me,
How often I've wondered where she can be.

————

There they mellow and there they brown,
Homely objects to folks from town;
Only some apples hung to dry
And doomed to be finally tombed in a pie.

ONLY HELD HIS OWN

Now there's Hezekiah Adams — nicest man you
    ever saw!
Never had a row with no one; never once got
    into law;
Always worked like thunderation, but to save
    his blessed life
Never seemed to get forehanded — and I've laid
    it to his wife,
For she always kept him meechin'; calls him
    down with sour tone,
Till the critter hasn't gumption for to say his
    soul's his own.
T'other day
Happened to ride along his way;
Heseki',
Like a gingham rag hung out to dry,
Peak-ed and pale,
Lopped on the gate 'cross the upper rail.
"Howdy!" says I,
"Blamed if I know," says Heseki'.
"Don't feel sick,
But marm's kept my back on a big hot brick
Till I can't tell
Whuther I'm ailin' or whuther I'm well."
"Think," says I,
"It's too early to hoe when the ground's so dry?"

Says he, " 'Bout all
I'm sartin' of is, I shall dig come fall."
Says I, " Things look
Like we farmers can fatten the pocket-book."
" Mebbe," says he,
" But marm vows there ain't much she can see."
" Ye can't jest crawl,"
Says I, "but there's money for folks with
    sprawl."
Old Hezekiah shifted legs and give a lonesome
    groan ;
" I begun with these two hands," said he,
" And I've only held my own."

He has always worked like blazes, but has
    always seemed to fail ;
— Made his grabs at prancin' Fortune, but has
    caught the critter's tail ;
Never jumped and gripped the bridle — wouldn't
    darst to on his life ;
Always acts too blasted meechin' — and I've laid
    it to his wife.

GRAMPY SINGS A SONG

Row-diddy, dow de, my little sis,
Hush up your teasin' and listen to this:
'Tain't much of a jingle, 'tain't much of a tune,
But it's spang-fired truth about Chester Cahoon.

The thund'rinest fireman Lord ever made
Was Chester Cahoon of the Tuttsville Brigade.
He was boss of the tub and the foreman of hose;
When the 'larm rung he'd start, sis, a-sheddin'
    his clothes,
— Slung cote and slung wes'cote and kicked off
    his shoes,
A-runnin' like fun, for he'd no time to lose.
And he'd howl down the ro'd in a big cloud of
    dust,
For he made it his brag he was allus there fust.
— Allus there fust, with a whoop and a shout,
And he never shut up till the fire was out.
And he'd knock out the winders and save all the
    doors,
And tear off the clapboards, and rip up the
    floors,
For he allus allowed 'twas a tarnation sin
To 'low 'em to burn, for you'd want 'em agin.
He gen'rally stirred up the most of his touse
In hustling to save the outside of the house.

And after he'd wrassled and hollered and pried,
He'd let up and tackle the stuff 'twas inside.
To see him you'd think he was daft as a loon,
But that was jest habit with Chester Cahoon.

Row diddy-iddy, my little sis,
Now see what ye think of a doin' like this:
The time of the fire at Jenkins' old place
It got a big start — was a desprit case;
The fambly they didn't know which way to turn.
And by gracious, it looked like it all was to burn.
But Chester Cahoon — oh, that Chester Cahoon,
He sailed to the roof like a reg'lar balloon;
Donno how he done it, but done it he did,
— Went down through the scuttle and shet
    down the lid.
And five minutes later that critter he came
To the second floor winder surrounded by
    flame.
He lugged in his arms, sis, a stove and a bed,
And balanced a bureau right square on his head.
His hands they was loaded with crockery stuff,
China and glass; as if that warn't enough,
He'd rolls of big quilts round his neck like a
    wreath,
And carried Mis' Jenkins' old aunt with his
    teeth.

You're right — gospel right, little sis, — didn't
   seem
The critter'd git down, but he called for the
   stream.
And when it comes strong and big round as my
   wrist
He stuck out his legs, sis, and give 'em a
   twist;
And he hooked round the water jes' if 'twas a
   rope
And down he come easin' himself on the slope,
— So almighty spry that he made that 'ere
   stream
As fit for his pupp'us' as if 'twas a beam.
Oh, the thund'rinest fireman Lord ever made
Was Chester Cahoon of the Tuttsville Brigade.

UNCLE MICAJAH STROUT

Guess that more'n a dozen lawyers, off and on,
from time to time,
Tried to settle down in Hudson, but they
couldn't earn a dime.
Never got a speck of business, never had a single
case,
Said they never in their travels struck so
blummed-blammed funny place.
People did a lot of hustling, town was flourish-
ing enough,
— Everybody but the lawyers had his fingers
full of stuff.
Lawyers stayed till they got hungry, then they'd
pull their shingles down
And go tearing off to somewhere, damning right
and left the town.
Told the lawyers round the county, " Hudson's
bound to starve you out
Till some patriot up and poisons one old cuss
down there named Strout.
    'Cause they won't fork up a fee,
    Long's he's round to referee.
    'Case of difference or doubt
    Folks say, ' Wal, we'll leave her out
        To Uncle Micajah Strout.' "

If a farmer bought a heifer and she didn't run
    to milk,
If a dickerer in horse trades struck a snag or
    tried to bilk,
If two parties got to haggling over what a farm
    was worth,
Or if breeders split in squabbling over weight or
    age or girth;
If a stubborn line-fence quarrel, right-of-way dis-
    pute, or deed,
Claim of heirship or of debtor, honest error,
    biassed greed,
Rose to foster litigation, no one scurried to the law,
No one belched out objurgations, sputtered oaths,
    or threatened war,
For there was a ready resource in a certain plain
    old gent,
Unassuming, blunt, and honest. When he said
    a thing it went.
So there was no chance for wrangle, disputations,
    snarls, or fray,
When the people of the village universally could
      say,

       " Oh, what's the use to fuss ?
       We shall only make a muss.
       We can fix it in about
       Half a minute. Leave it out
         To Uncle Micajah Strout."

So no wonder all the lawyers banned and cursed
   the place, and left;
For contention was but fleeting and the town
   was never cleft
By a quarrel or dissension. Rows were always
   settled young
By the pacifying magic of Micajah's ready
   tongue.
When at last his days were ended and he passed
   — well, now you bet
That he had the biggest funeral ever seen in
   Somerset.
Miss him? Guess we miss Micajah, but if ever
   dreams come true,
I've a sort of sneaking notion that he hasn't yet
   got through
Settling things for us in Hudson; for I dreamed
   — and this is straight —
That I died and went to Heaven, but was yanked
   up at the gate.
Peter showed me facts and figures, all the
   records, and allowed
That I'd have to take my chances down below
   with t'other crowd;
— Said the thing was pretty even, but he had to
   draw it fine,
Then commenced to hunt the index for the next
   shade in the line.

I protested, and we had it, this and that, and pro
and con,
And I hung and begged and argued when he
told me to move on.
Till at last he called a cherub, sent the little
chap inside,
Owning up that he was bothered as to how he
should decide.
  " But I'll give you all the show
  That I can," said he. " You know,
  I've arranged, in case of doubt,
  — When it's close, — to leave it out
  To Uncle Micajah Strout."

THE TRUE STORY OF A KICKER

There lived two frogs, so I've been told,
    In a quiet wayside pool;
And one of those frogs was a blamed bright frog,
    But the other frog was a fool.

Now a farmer man with a big milk can
    Was wont to pass that way;
And he used to stop and add a drop
    Of the *aqua* pure, they say.

And it chanced one morn in the early dawn,
    When the farmer's sight was dim,
He scooped those frogs in the water he dipped,
    — Which same was a joke on him.

The fool frog sank in the swashing tank
    As the farmer bumped to town.
But the smart frog flew like a tug-boat screw,
    And he swore he'd not go down.

So he kicked and splashed and he slammed and
      thrashed,
    And he kept on top through all;
And he churned that milk in first-class shape
    In a great big butter ball.

Now when the milkman got to town,
  And opened the can, there lay
The fool frog drowned ; but, hale and sound,
  The kicker he hopped away.

MORAL.

Don't fret your life with needless strife,
  Yet let this teaching stick :
You'll find, old man, in the world's big can
  It sometimes pays to kick.

ZEK'L PRATT'S HARRYCANE

'Twould make an ox curl up and die
To hear how Zek'l Pratt would lie.
  — Why, that blamed Zeke
  Could hardly speak
Without he'd let some whopper fly.
Come jest as natchrul to him, too,
  — 'Twas innocent, and them as knew
Zeke's failin's never took great stock,
But jest stood back and let him talk;
Jest let him thrash his peck o' charf,
Then got behind his back to laugh.
Why, Zeke would — jest hold on and see
What that old liar told to me.

Last fall while gettin' in his grain
He said he see'd a harrycane
  — A cikerloon, as they say West —
A-boomin' on like all possesst.
And Zekel see'd to his consarn
'Twas bound plumb straight for his new barn.

" 'Twas crickitul," says he. " Thinks I,
I've got to be almighty spry.
If somethin' ain't done kind o' brash
That barn will get chawed inter hash.
It don't take long for me to think,
And what I done was quicker'n wink.

Jest gafflin' up a couple boards
I sashayed out deerectly to'ards
That howlin', growlin' harrycane
That come a-raisin' merry Cain.

"When I'd got out as fur's my wind
Would take me, I slacked up and shinned
That cob-piled monnyment o' stones
Between my land and Bial Jones.
    Though I don't scare
    I'll own, I swear,
It sent a twitter through my bones
When I got where that I could see
The thing 'twas goin' to tackle me.
'Twas big and round and blacker'n Zip,
— And powerful? My sakes, 'twould grip
A tree or barn or line o' fence
And make 'em look like thirty cents.
While all the time it growled and chawed
And spit the slivers forty rod.
— As things looked then a bob-tailed darn
Was too much price for Pratt's new barn.

"But let me tell ye this, my son,
Me'n them boards warn't there for fun.
I held one underneath each arm ;
    The ends stuck out
    In front about

Ten feet. I held 'em aidge to aidge
And made a fust-class kind of wedge.
I grit my teeth. There was a calm
For jest a minit, kind o' 's ef
That harrycane had stopped itse'f
And snickered, snorted, laughed, and yelled,
Then stopped again and sort o' held
Its breath ; then swellin' up its breast
Swooped down to knock me galley-west.

" It grabbed them boards and then 'twas fight !
But scare me ? Not a gol-durned mite !
It pulled and tugged and yanked and hauled
And tooted, howled, and squealed and squalled ;
It picked up sculch and dirt, and threw,
And followed with a tree or two ;
It hit me with a rotten squash,
And give me fits with Marm Jones' wash.
But 'twarn't no use, suh, Zek'l Pratt
Ain't built to scare at things like that.
I jest let into that air tyke
And punched its innards reg'lar-like
With them 'ere boards, and honest true,
I split her square and plumb in two.
One half went yowlin' by to right
And one to left — and out of sight.
While Zek'l Pratt was still on deck
With Marm Jones' night-gown round his neck."

THOSE PICKLES OF MARM'S

It doesn't need eyesight to tell that it's fall,
    Up here in Maine.
Though the glamor of yellow is over it all,
    And the cold, swishing rain
Comes peltering down and goes stripping the
    leaves,
And smokes in cold spray from the edge of the
    eaves.
Ah, it's wild out of doors, but come in here with
    me
Where mother's as busy as busy can be.
And you need not your eyes, sir, to know it is fall
In this stifle and stirring and steam like a pall.
For there's savor of spices and odorous charms
When your nose gets a sniff of these pickles of
    marm's.

You know it is fall without using your eyes,
    Up here in Maine.
There is fragrance that floats as the flower-pot
    dies
    In the tears of the rain.
And the hand of the frost strips the sheltering
    leaves
From the pumpkins, those bombs of the sentinel
    sheaves

That stiffly and starkly keep guard in the field,
A desolate rank without weapon or shield.
And the fragrance of death like a delicate musk
Floats up from the field through the crispness of
    dusk;
Yet out from the kitchen, more savory far,
Drifts the fragrance of pickles compounded by
    ma.

The autumn sweeps past like a dame to a ball,
    Up here in Maine.
Her perfumes would stagger shy Springtime, but
    Fall,
    Like a matron of Spain,
Puts musk in her bosom and scent on her hair,
And prinks her gay robe with elaborate care.
Yet the fragrance she sheds has the savor of
    death,
The brain is turned giddy beneath her fierce
    breath,
Till over it all floats the vigorous scent
Of spices and hot things and good things, all
    blent;
It's wonderful, friend, how it tickles and calms,
— That whiff from those simmering pickles of
    marm's.

"THE MAN I KNEW I KILLED"

Ezra Saunders, of Hopkins' Creek,
Was the next old soldier asked to speak.
He'd seen his share of the thousands slain
In the active days of the Umteenth Maine;
And we settled back to hear him tell
His reasons for thinking that "War is Hell."

"Dear comrades of Keesuncook Post and ladies
  of the Corps,
I thank you for this invite and I'm proud to
  take the floor.
I was thinkin' as I set here of the battles that
  I've fought,
Of the suff'rin' and the slaughter — and the
  sudden, awful thought
Come across me that I'd taken very likely scores
  of lives,
— Taken fathers from their children, taken
  husbands from their wives.
While mad with heat of battle I was pumping
  reeking lead,
Not knowing, no, nor caring, where the bullet
  found its bed.
Now people they will ask us if we really, truly
  know
For a fact that while a-fightin' we have ever
  killed a foe.

But it's rare you find a soldier who has seen, in
  heat of strife,
That the bullet he had fired was the one to take
  a life.
Now, to-night, I'm going to tell you, though I
  hate to, boys, I swan,
That I know I've done my murder; that I *know*
  I've killed my man.

" 'Twas when we got our rapping at the fight of
  Hatcher's Run;
I was running hard as any; — yes, I threw away
  my gun
And the rest of my equipment, and proceeded,
  friends, to steer
Just as fast as legs would help me for protection
  at the rear.
I was quite a nervy sprinter — 'bout as swift as
  you will find,
But I couldn't shake that Johnny who came
  slammin' on behind;
For he had the Georgy straddle and was sort of
  razor-edged,
And if nothin' special busted, I was spoke for,
  so I jedged.
He was hanging to his rifle, but he didn't try to
  shoot,
— He see he had me solid, — but I give the
  blame galoot

A standard mile or such-like and had druv him
    'in the list,'
When I stepped upon a hubble, fell, and give
    my leg a twist.
And the tumble sort of stunned me so I laid
    there quite a spell,
Expectin' that he'd grab me; just a-harkin' for
    his yell.
But things stayed calm and quiet, so I peeked;
    he laid there sprawled
'Bout a dozen yards behind me. And he looked
    so queer I crawled
Slowly back to reconnoitre, got where I could
    see his head,
Saw his face was black's a stove-pipe. Apo-
    plexy! He was dead.
And I stood and wept above him, stirred, dear
    comrades, to the peth
With the awful, awful pity for that man I'd run
    to death.
And my conscience always pricked me and my
    heart with grief is filled,
For there ain't no question, comrades, there's a
    man I know I killed."

'LONG SHORE

CRUISE OF THE "NANCY P."

We was off Seguin with the " Nancy P.,"
  From the Sheepscot bound for Boston way;
We was one day out, and massy me !
  What a leak she'd sprung sence she left the bay !
    Why, never knowed sech an awful leak,
    Gad, we made her old pump squeak,
    Gad, we made it whoop and hump,
      — Two at a turn, on the stiddy jump, —
        Ker-chonk, ker-chump,
With an up yo-ho and a down ker-bump.

But the more we pumped, the more she drawed,
  And we all turned to for a mighty pull;
But when we giv' her the soundin' rawd,
  Why, bless yer soul, she was jam, bang full.
    Plumb, jamb full to the soaked old deck,
    Full to her gol-durned tarred old neck ;
    Wonder was how she kept aflo't,
      With the sea a-gozzlin' in her thro't ;
        Ker-do't, ker-do't,
— And we couldn't leave, 'cause there warn't no
  bo't.

So we hung to the pump and we giv' her Cain,
  Though it didn't seem to be no use.
We thought of the good dry ground in Maine,
  And durned the pelt of that old caboose,

Durned the hide of a tops'l tub,
For we never thought we'd see the Hub;
— Got so scart we forgot to thank
Our lucky stars for a lo'd of plank,
Ker-chink, ker-chank,
And still we bounced that old pump crank.

So we woggled on like a bale of hay,
And we set our teeth and we pumped with
groans.
At last we got to Boston bay;
But our arms were stretched to our ankle bones,
Hands were the size of corn-fed hams,
Eyes bulged out like the horns o' rams,
We humped like monkeys bound for war,
And ev'ry man had a raw, red paw,
Ker-haw, ker-haw,
We beached that tub — and then we saw —

The "Nancy P.," she'd grown that old,
Her butts had rotted all away.
Her lo'd of planks still jammed the hold,
But we'd left her bottom in Sheepscot bay.
So there we'd made a turrible try
To pump old 'Lantic ocean dry.
Over our rail, 'twixt you and me,
We'd h'isted, suttin, a mile of sea;
Blame me!   But we
Was a darn sick crowd on the "Nancy P."

"We was off Seguin with the 'Nancy P.'"

TALE OF THE SEA-FARING MAN

I purchased a glass of stiff Maine grog for a
    salty son of the sea,
And he confidentially leaned on the bar and
    spun this yarn for me:

" 'Twas down in the aidge of the Saragos' in the
    nineteenth latitood
That I think I see the dumdest sight that ever a
    sailor viewed.

" We was dobbin' along with dumpy sails in a
    nigh-about dead calm,
When the forrard watch give a good long squint,
    and he yapped a loud alarm.

" And there afloat, two points to port, was a
    shark, a reg'lar he 'un,
The biggest shark I've ever seen outside the
    Caribbeun.

" The old man reckoned he'd have his pelt, and
    he yelled to the second mate,
'Sling over the biggest hook ye've got, with a
    good big plug o' bait.'

" We dragged her astern and his nobs come on,
    and then with a mighty splosh,
He gulped the pork, he bit the rope; and away
    he went, by gosh!

"But when he'd hipered two miles to lee, and
  begun to wopse and wheel,
We figgered he found the lunch he had a rayther
  too hearty meal.

"Yet right behind the quarter wash the critter
  swum next day,
And though he gobbled the bait we threw, he
  allus got away.

"And at last, do ye know, we liked the cuss for
  the way he showed his spunk,
And we named him Pete, and shared salt hoss,
  and tossed him a daily junk.

"He got the orts of the fish we caught and, all
  in all, I'll bet
A two-hoss waggin wouldn't haul the stuff that
  critter et.

"Then one day Jones, the heftiest man we had
  in all the crew,
Went off the rail with a swinging sail, and Pete
  he et him too.

"From that time on we tipped our caps to the
  razor-backed old brute,
— We tipped our caps and pulled a bow in a
  most profound salute;

" For 'twas only due from a decent crew to honor
    a comrade's grave,
Though 'twas odd, I'll own, to have a tomb afloat
    on the ocean wave.

" And the old man ordered the fish lines coiled,
    for he 'lowed 'twarn't proper game
To bob behind for a grave-yard lot; so Pete
    swum on the same,

" — Swum on the same, though we come to see
    that he didn't act quite right.
For he grew as thin's a belayin' pin on that gol-
    durned appetite.

" And we couldn't figger the secret out, though
    the second mate was firm
That stowed 'tween decks in the shark's insides
    was a bastin' big tape-worm.

" As we didn't have no vermifuge we could only
    mourn for Pete,
And steal salt hoss when the mate warn't round,
    and give him lots to eat.

" But at last he rolled his glassy eyes and give
    an awful churn,
And turned his belly up to view and drifted off
    astern.

" He rolled and sogged on a logy swell like a
nut-cake dropped in fat,
And it 'peared to all there was suthin' wrong
with the shark we was lookin' at.

"So the old man ordered the gig crew up, and
the bos'n piped a tune,
And away we sploshed with the mate ahead
a-grippin' a big harpoon.

" He slung the thing when we drew abreast and
we backed like all-possessed ;
But the shark was sleepin' sound, you bet, for
we never broke his rest.

" — We never broke his peaceful snooze, though
plunk to the eyelet head
Went rippin' in that big harpoon, — for, you see,
the shark was dead.

" And the old man ordered an ortopsy, for the
thing seemed mighty queer
That an able-bodied, hearty shark was deader'n
a door-knob here.

"So the mate was medical 'xaminer, and he
straddled the critter's back
And laid him open from deck to keel with one
almighty whack.

"Now listen close while I tell the rest, for this is
   the story's peth,
— You may take my nob for a scuttle-butt if
   the shark warn't starved to death.

"Starved to death, though the sea was full of
   the fattest kind of fish,
— Starved, though a seaman plump and sound
   had tumbled in his dish,

"— Starved though he had in his gorged insides
   I'll bet a hundredweight
Of every kind of a floating thing from codfish
   down to bait.

"And this was how: He'd spied, we judged, an
   empty cask afloat,
And bein' a glutten he grabbed the thing and
   tucked it down his throat.

"The cask, we found, had an open end — the
   bottom was good and stout
— The shark had swallowed the whole end fust
   — the open end was out.

"And ev'ry mossel the critter et was scooped by
   the cask inside;
His vittles failed to reach the spot, and so the
   poor shark died."

This is a sample of weird, wild yarns the marin-
   ers relate
Under the spur of a glass of grog in a Prohibi-
   tion State.

CAP'N NUTTER OF THE "PUDDENTAME"

The foam bells tinkle at gilded prow
— There's a creamy wake to the far horizon.
And she tiptoes along with a New York bow
To the curt'sying waves, and we'll all allow,
  She's the daintiest yacht we have set our eyes
   on.
   While sneaking after, in grimy shame,
   Rolls tops'l schooner, the " Puddentame."

On the rocking surge swings the millionaire,
  And about him splendor and music and
   laughter;
The glint of jewels and ladies fair;
Jollity throned, and Old King Care
  Drowned in the brine and dragging after.
   But the billows lift and toss the same
   Old Cap'n Nutter in the " Puddentame."

Under the gloom of the Porcupines,
  In the gleam of the lights of the summer city,
In a tapestried cabin the rich man dines,
And toasts his friends in his bubbling wines,
  While the repartee and the careless ditty
   Float from the lips of squire and dame
   To Cap'n Nutter of the " Puddentame."

And the old man munches his bread and cheese
  In the gloom and grime of his little cuddy;
— Through the mirk of the dusty deadlight sees
This riot of riches; then on his knees
    — This sea-stained, warped old fuddy-duddy —
      He prays for their souls in the Saviour's
        name,
        — Does Cap'n Nutter of the " Puddentame."

And they? — Why, they neither know nor care
  That the honest chap has knelt and pleaded.
For just at the edge of the dazzling glare
From the rocking yacht of the millionaire,
    The old craft swings and sways unheeded.
      Yet who'll sleep better, jaded Fame
      Or Cap'n Nutter of the " Puddentame " ?

GOOD–BY, LOBSTER

We've gazed with resignation on the passing of
the auk,
Nor care a continental for the legendary rok ;
And the dodo and the bison and the ornith-o-
rhyn-chus
May go and yet their passing brings no shade of
woe to us.
We entertain no sorrow that the megatherium
Forever and forever is departed, dead and
dumb:
But a woe that hovers o'er us brings a keen and
bitter pain
As we weep to see the lobster vanish off the
coast of Maine.

Oh, dear crustacean dainty of the dodge-holes
of the sea,
I tune my lute in minor in a threnody for thee.
You've been the nation's martyr and 'twas wrong
to treat you so,
And you may not think we love you; yet we
hate to see you go.
We've given you the blazes and hot-potted you,
and yet
We've loved you better martyred than when
living, now you bet.

You have no ears to listen, so, alas, we can't
    explain
The sorrow that you bring us as you leave the
    coast of Maine.

Do you fail to mark our feeling as we bitterly
    deplore
The passing of the hero of the dinner at the
    shore?
Ah, what's the use of living if you also can't
    survive
Until you die to furnish us the joy of one
    " broiled live " ?
And what can e'er supplant you as a cold dish
    on the side ?
Or what assuage our longings when to salads
    you're denied ?
Or what can furnish thunder to the legislative
    brain
When ruthless Fate has swept you from the rocky
    coast of Maine ?

I see, and sigh in seeing, in some distant, future
    age
Your varnished shell reposing under glass upon
    a stage,
The while some pundit lectures on the curios of
    the past,

And dainty ladies shudder as they gaze on you
    aghast.
And all the folks that listen will wonder vaguely
    at
The fact that once lived heathen who could eat
    a Thing like that.
Ah, that's the fate you're facing — but laments
    are all in vain
— Tell the dodo that you saw us when you
    lived down here in Maine.

CURE FOR HOMESICKNESS

She wrote to her daddy in Portland, Maine, from
out in Denver, Col.,
And she wrote, alas, despondently that life had
commenced to pall;
And this was a woful, woful case, for she was
a six months' bride
Who was won and wed in the State of Maine by
the side of the bounding tide.
And ah, alack, she was writing back that she
longed for Portland, Maine,
Till oh, her feelings had been that wrenched she
could hardly stand the strain!
Though her hubby dear was still sincere, she
sighed the livelong day
For a good old sniff of the sewers and salt from
the breast of Casco bay.
And she wrote she sighed, and she said she'd
cried, and her appetite fell off,
And she'd grown as thin's a belaying-pin, with a
terrible hacking cough;
And she sort of hinted that pretty soon she'd
start on a reckless scoot
And hook for her home in Portland, Maine, by
the very shortest route.
But her daddy dear was a man of sense, and he
handles fish wholesale,

And he sat and fanned himself awhile with a
   big broad codfish tail;

And he recollected the way he felt when he
   dwelt in the World's Fair whirl.

He slapped his head. "By hake," he said, "I
   know what ails that girl."

And he went to a ten-cord pile of cod and he
   pulled the biggest out,

A jib-shaped critter, broad's a sail, — three feet
   from tail to snout.

And he pasted a sheet of postage stamps from
   snout clear down to tail,

Put on a quick delivery stamp, and sent the cod
   by mail.

She smelled it a-coming two blocks off on the
   top of the postman's pack;

She rushed to meet him, and scared him blind by
   climbing the poor man's back.

But she got the fish, bit out a hunk, ate postage
   stamps and all,

And a happy wife in a happy home lives out in
   Denver, Col.

ON THE OLD COAST TUB

Blast from the winter. Wrack-wood and splinter
  Adrift in the smother of roaring lee shore :
And a blunt-nosed old coaster; some ancient
    sea-wagon,
    Sweeps in from the fog no more — no more,
      Rolls in from the sea no more.

————

Bricks make her load and New York her destin-
    ation.
  (Dern yer hide, ye snoozer, keep a-pumping
    there, I say!)
Bricks for a cargo and she leaks like thundera-
    tion,
    And the gulls a-trailin' after like the buzzards
      sniffin' prey!
        Pump away!
And ev'ry brick a-soakin' in her innards growls
    and grates ;
    She hesitates — she balks and waits,
    And holy hawse-pipe, how she hates
      To leave Penobscot Bay !

Pounce ! On her bows leap the combers like
    a tiger-cat,
  (Lift 'er on the handle, there, you loafer,
    pump away!)

Lurch! Reels her gait, and her sloshin' scup-
    pers hiccup at
  The sight of drunken breakers fightin' past
    'er up the bay.
        Pump, I say!
Oh, give her all the rotten sail her leary masts
    will lug.
  Ka-chig, ka-chug; her ugly mug
  Rolls orkord as a driftin' jug,
      And so we slosh away.

Grub to last a week, a quadrant and an alma-
    nick;
  (Wag 'er there, you rascal, wag 'er lively
    there, I say!)
Rotten are her sails and her hold a-roar with
    shiftin' brick,
  — Ain't we up ag'inst it if a norther comes
    our way?
        Pump, I say!
Stagger down, ye bloated drunkard, wheel and
    take the starboard tack!
  Ka-slup, ka-smack, now work 'er back,
  Jest hear that old black canvas crack.
      Ho! Davy Jones, hooray!

———

Black cordage tangled, dead features mangled,
  Adrift in the smother of roaring lee shore.

And a blunt-nosed old coaster; some broad-
    bellied wagon
Sweeps in from the sea no more — no more,
    — Rolls in from the sea no more.

TALE OF THE KENNEBEC MARINER

Guess I've never told you, sonny, of the strandin'
  and the wreck
Of the steamboat " Ezry Johnson " that run up
  the Kennebec.
That was 'fore the time of steam-cars, and the
  " Johnson " filled the bill
On the route between Augusty and the town of
  Waterville.

She was built old-fashined model, with a
  bottom's flat's your palm,
With a paddle-wheel behind her, druv' by one
  great churnin' arm.
Couldn't say that she was speedy — sploshed
  along and made a touse,
But she couldn't go much faster than a man
  could tow a house.
Still, she skipped and skived tremendous, dodged
  the rocks and skun the shoals,
In a way the boats of these days couldn't do to
  save their souls.
Didn't draw no 'mount of water, went on top
  instead of through.
This is how there come to happen what I'm going to tell to *you*.

— Hain't no need to keep you guessing, for I
    know you won't suspect
How that thunderin' old " Ez. Johnson " ever
    happened to get wrecked.

She was overdue one ev'nin', fog come down
    most awful thick ;
'Twas about like navigating round inside a
    feather tick.
Proper caper was to anchor, but she seemed to
    run all right,
And we humped her — though 'twas resky —
    kept her sloshing through the night.

Things went on all right till morning, but along
    'bout half-past three
Ship went dizzy, blind, and crazy — waves
    seemed wust I ever see.
Up she went and down she scuttered ; sometimes
    seemed to stand on end,
Then she'd wallopse, sideways, cross-ways, in a
    way, by gosh, to send
Shivers down your spine. She'd teeter, fetch a
    spring, and take a bounce,
Then squat down, sir, on her haunches with a
    most je-roosly jounce.
Folks got up and run a-screaming, forced the
    wheelhouse, grabbed at me,

— Thought we'd missed Augusty landin' and
    had gone plum out to sea.

— Fairly shot me full of questions, but I said
    'twas jest a blow;

Still, that didn't seem to soothe 'em, for there
    warn't no wind, you know!

Yas, sir, spite of all that churnin', warn't a whis-
    per of a breeze

— No excuse for all that upset and those strange
    and dretful seas.

Couldn't spy a thing around us — every way
    'twas pitchy black,

And I couldn't seem to comfort them poor crit-
    ters on my back.

Couldn't give 'em information, for 'twas dark's
    a cellar shelf;

— Couldn't tell 'em nothing 'bout it — for I
    didn't know myself.

So I gripped the " Johnson's " tiller, kept the
    rudder riggin' taut,

Kept a-praying, chawed tobacker, give her steam,
    and let her swat.

Now, my friend, jest listen stiddy: when the sun
    come out at four,

We warn't tossin' in the breakers off no stern
    and rockbound shore;

But I'd missed the gol-durned river, and I swow
    this 'ere is true,
I had sailed eight miles 'cross country in a heavy
    autumn dew.
There I was clear up in Sidney, and the tossings
    and the rolls
Simply happened 'cause we tackled sev'ral miles
    of cradle knolls.
Sun come out and dried the dew up; there she
    was a stranded wreck,
And they soaked me eighteen dollars' cartage to
    the Kennebec.

DRIVE, CAMP, AND WANGAN

THE LAW 'GAINST SPIKE–SOLE BOOTS

It's a case of scuff in your stocking-feet, from
    Seboomook down, my hearties ;
Sling your spikers around your neck and swear
    your way to town.
The dudes that we sent to legislate, and figger
    at balls and parties,
Have tinkered the laws to suit themselves, and
    they've done us good and brown.

There's a howl, you bet, from the Medway dam
    across to the Caucmogummac,
For the laws came up in the tote-team mail, and
    we've got the new statoots,
And of all the things that was ever planned to
    give us a gripe in the stomach,
The worst is the corker that t'runs us down for
    a-wearin' our old calked boots.

You can't chank on to a hotel floor,
You've got to leave calked boots at the door.
They make ye peel your hucks in the street
And walk to the bar in your stocking-feet.

It's a blank of a note that a man with chink
Can't prance to the rail and get his drink,
But it's five and costs if ye mar the paint,
And ten if the feller that makes complaint

Gets mad at a playful push in the eyes
And goes into court with a lot of lies.
It's ten if ye sliver a steam-bo't's deck
— There ain't no argue — it's right in the neck.
And they soak you, too, on the railroad train ;
— Why, there's hardly a loggin' crew in Maine
But what has claimed, as a nat'ral right,
A chance to holler and beller and fight,
And knock the stuffin' out of the seats,
Rip off the blinds and club with the cleats.
But now if the bloomin' brakeman talks,
And you vaccinate him once with calks ;
If you feel like a man with a royal flush
And, jest for the joke of it, rip some plush,
Oh, they take that law and they peel you sore ;
You pay for the damage, and ten plunks more.
'Tain't much like the days when we had some
    rights,
When we roosters sharpened our spurs in fights,
When never a crowd put up galoots
That could scrap with the fellers with spike-sole
    boots.

————

It's a case of step to the wangan camp, and buy
    some partent leathers ;
And go a-snoopin' along to town like a dude on
    his weddin'-trip ;
And the only thing you can do to a guy is to tickle
    his nose with feathers,

And curl in your seats in the smokin'-car when
    a drummer gives you lip.
There was fun, by gee, in the good old days
    when we whooped 'er into the city,
And you trailed our way by the slivers we left
    from the railroad down to the dives,
And we owned the town where we left our cash ;
    and now it's a thunderin' pity
If all of a sudden you've grown too good for the
    boys who are off the drives.

Oh, make the laws, go make the laws with your
    derned old Legislature,
Jest give us orders to wear plug hats and come
    down in full dress suits.
We'll wear the togs ; but give us spikes, or
    you've busted the laws of nature,
For angels can just as well shed wings as a
    driver his spike-sole boots.

THE CHAP THAT SWINGS THE AXE

Sing a song of paper; first the tall, straight
  spruce,
Torn from off the mountains for the roaring
  presses' use.
— A shrieking laceration by the "barker" and
  the saw;
A slow, grim maceration in the grinder's grum-
  bling maw;
A dizzy dash through calenders and over whirring rolls,
— And the press can smut the paper so's to save
  or damn your souls;
The press has got the paper, it can give you lies
  or facts
— That vexes not the fellow up in Maine who
  swings the axe.

————

   Chock!
        Chock!
                Chock!
The throb stuttered up from the heart of the
  wood,
Erratic and faint, yet the trees understood,
— Though distant and dull like the tick of a
  clock
It started a tremor through all the great flock.

King Spruce was a-shiver and rooted with dread,
While past him to safety the wood people fled ;
The fox with his muzzle turned backward to
  snuff
The bear trundling on like an animate muff,
And rabbits up-ending in wonder and fright,
Then scudding once more with the others in
  flight.
Yet that which has reason most urgent to flee
Stands grim in the rout of the panic — the
  Tree !
While up the long slope, glaring red 'gainst the
  snow, —
His shirt of the hue of the butcher, — the foe,
Beating fierce at the trunks with relentless
  attacks,
Comes on to the slaughter, the Man with the Axe.
    Chock !
            Chock !
                    Chock !
    Shudder and totter and shiver and rock !
    — Pygmy assailing with dull steady knock.
    Trunk yawning wide with a hideous gash.
    Snow-covered limbs thrown a-sprawl; and
      then crash !
The pens and the presses are waiting, and eyes
That will glow with delight, or dilate with sur-
  prise.

For there in the heart of the spruce there is
  rolled
The fabric for thousands of stories untold.
And on the white paper may later be spread
The fall of a nation, or fame of one dead
Who now strides abroad in his health and suc-
  cess,
But will pass to the tomb when that log meets
  the press.
There under the bark of that spruce there is
  furled
A web that will carry the news of a world,
That clamors and crowds at the swaying red
  backs
Of the toilers of Maine, the rough men of the
  axe.

THE SONG OF THE WOODS'
DOG–WATCH

'Tis the weirdly witching hour of the woods'
" dog-watch,"
When the guide suspends the kettle in the ash
limb's crotch,
Stirs the drowsy, drowsy embers till the cozy
fire beams
And flickers dance like gnomes and elves athwart
the glowing dreams
Of the sleeping town-bred fisher who is stretched
with placid soul
On the earth in sweeter slumber than his town
couch can cajole.
Ah, 'tis tough on bone and muscle, is this chas-
ing after fun —
And a sleeper gets to sleeping forty knots along
'bout one.
But the guide is up a-stirring — monstrous shape
with flaring torch,
Prodding up the dozing fire for the woods' " dog-
watch."
And the slow unclosing eyelids of the startled
dreamer see
This dreadful apparition thrown in shadows on a
tree.
And his heart for just a second goes to skirrup-
ing about

As it flopped when he was wrestling with that
    five-three-quarter trout.
But the ogre leaves the shadows, leans against
    a handy tree
And remarks : " The water's bilin'; won't ye
    have a cup o' tea?"
And he wakes to a night of the fisherman's
    June,
— Afar the weird lilt of the dolorous loon
Floats up from the heart of the fair, velvet
    night—
A globule of sound winging slow in its flight.
As elfin a note as a gnome ever blew,
It wells from the waters, " Ah-loo-hoo-ah-hoo-
    o-o-o."
O spell of the forest ! O glimmer and gleam
From the sheen of the lake and the mist-breath-
    ing stream !
The night and the stars and the dolorous loon
Make mystic the spell of the fisherman's June.

The spruces sing the lyric of the wood's dog-
    watch ;
The kettle as it bubbles in the ash limb's crotch,
The rustle of the spindles of the hemlock and
    the pine,
The crackle where the licking tongues of ruddy
    fire twine,

"No woman's hand to make it home."

The oboe, in the distance, of the weird and lone-
    some loon,
— This chorus sings the lyric of the blessed
    month of June.

What June? Your June of meadows or your
    June of scented breeze,
Or your June begirt with roses stretched in
    hammock at her ease?
Such a deity for maidens! I can bow to no
    such June!
I extol the mystic goddess of the Forest's Silent
    Noon.
— Noon of day or noon of night-time — in the
    vast and silent deeps,
Where human care or human woe or human
    envy sleeps,
Where rugged depths surround me, dim and
    silent, deep and wide,
And no human shares my joy but that second
    self, my guide.
— Here's a June that one can worship. Here's
    a June by right a queen,
'Neath her hand eternal mountains, 'neath her
    feet eternal green.
And here will I adore her, seeking out her
    awful throne
With the Silence swimming round me, and
    alone, thank God, alone!

FIDDLER CURED THE CAMP

Wal, things they was deader'n old Billy-be-darn,
The boss was pernickity, cook wouldn't yarn;
For we'd heard ev'ry story old Beans had to spin,
And we hadn't no longin's to hear 'em agin;
Old Pitts, the head chopper, we'd pumped him
    out, too,
— And he swow'd that he'd sung ev'ry song
    that he knew.
As the rest wasn't gifted, a sort of a damp
Old glister of silence fell over Peel's camp.
The deacon-seat doldrums were blacker'n old Zip,
We'd set there an hour with never a yip,
'Cept the suckin' o' lips at the quackin' T.D.'s,
With the oof and the woo of the lonesome pine
    trees
W'istling over our smok'-hole. It grew on us,
    too;
Our thoughts got as thick an' as musty an' blue
As the cloud o' tobacker smoke, mixed with the
    steams
From the woolens that dried on the stringers
    and beams.
Old Attegat Peter said we was bewitched;
He said that he seed the Old Gal when she
    twitched
A fistful o' hair out the gray hosses' tail
For a-makin' witch tattin'. She'd hung on a nail

The queerisome web, so he said, an' the holes
— They were fifty — they stood for the whole
of our souls.

An' there we would swing, an' hang there we
must,
Till the hoodoo was busted. Eternally cussed,
So he said, was the buffle-brained feller that
dared
To touch the witch-web that was holding us
snared.

Aw, we didn't believe it — 'tain't like that we
did !
But still we warn't fussy ! If we could get
rid
Of the dumps by a charm, we was ready to try,
And Peter said singin' would knock 'em sky
high.
Wal, Peter said " singin' ; " I can't tell a lie,
'Twarn't singin', 'twarn't nothin' — that mourn-
ful ki-yi !
That seemed like a beller in ev'ry man's boot,
An' 'twarn't none surprisin' the witch didn't
scoot.
So there did we set in a stew an' a cloud,
A grumpy old, lumpy old dob of a crowd.

But oh, landsy sake a-Peter, when the fiddle come
       to camp,
    W'y you wouldn't know the place:
    — Wuz a grin on ev'ry face
W'en we know'd the critter'd got it.   An' it
    reely seemed the lamp
Had a 'lectric light attachment; an' you
    oughter heard us stamp
When that feller took his fiddle out an' rosined
       up the bow.
    Then he yawked an' yeaked an' yawked
    'Twistin' keys ontil she squawked,
An' we set there jest a-gawpin'; not a word to
    say, but, oh,
We was right on pins an' needles fer to have
    him let 'er go.

Tweedle-weedle, yeaky, yawky, 'nother twist,
       an' pretty soon
    He was waitin' to begin,
    With 'er underneath his chin;
He a-askin', all a-grinnin', " Wall, boys, name
    it; what's your tune?"
An' we hollered all in concert, " Whoop 'er up
    on ' Old Zip Coon'!"

Oh, the deacon-seat had cushions an' the bunks
    were stuffed with down,

While the feller sawed the strings;
We could feel our sproutin' wings,
An' we wanted to go soarin', go a-sailin', wear a
crown,
Tear the ground up, whoop-ta-ra-ra, mix some
red and paint the town.

Oh, he played the "Lights o' London" an' he
played "The Devil's Dream,"
— All the old ones — played 'em all;
Rode right on 'er — made 'er squall;
Didn't stop to semi-quiver, tip-toe Nancy, pass
the cream;
No; he let 'er go Jerooshy, clear the track an'
lots o' steam.

Thought I'd never heerd such playin' sence the
Lord had giv' me breath
An' that P. I. — seems as if
He could put the bang an' biff
In the chitter of a cat-gut like to touch the very
peth
In yer marrow; like to raise yer from the very
jaws of death.

So, oh, landsy sake a-Peter, when that fiddle
come our way,

Say, you wouldn't know the place,
— Wus a grin on ev'ry face.
— Went to workin' like the blazes an' our vittles
set — an' say,
Guess the Hoodoo flew to thunder when the
Haw-Haw come to stay.

THE SONG OF THE SAW

The song is the shriek of the strong that are
  slain,
— The monarchs that people the woodlands of
  Maine;
  — 'Tis the cry of a merciless war.
And it echoes by river, by lake, and by stream,
Wherever saws scream or the bright axes gleam,
— 'Tis keyed to the sibilant rush of the steam,
  And the song is the song of the saw.

Come stand in the gloom of this clamorous
  room,
Where giants groan past us a-drip from the
  boom,
Borne here from the calm of the forest and hill,
— Aghast at the thunderous roar of the mill,
At rumble of pulley and grumble of shaft
And the tumult and din of the sawyer's rude
  craft.

Stand here in the ebb of the riotous blast,
As the saw's mighty carriage goes thundering
  past,
One man at the lever and one at the dog.
The slaughter is bloodless and senseless the
  log,

Yet the anguish of death and the torment of
hell
Are quavering there in the long, awful yell,
That shrills above tumult of gearing and wheel
As the carriage rolls down and the timber meets
steel.

Scream! And a board is laid bare for a home.
Shriek! And a timber for mansion and dome,
For the walls of a palace, or toil's homely use,
Is reft from the flanks of the prostrate King
Spruce.
And thus in the clamor of pulley and wheel,
In the plaint of the wood and the slash of the
steel,
Is wrought the undoing of Maine's sturdy lords,
— The martyrs the woodlands yield up to our
swords.
The song is the knell of these strong that are
slain,
The monarchs that people the woodlands of
Maine.
And the Fury that whirls in the din of this
war,
With rioting teeth and insatiable maw, is the
saw!
And this is the song of the saw.

DOWN THE TRAIL WITH GUM PACKS

Ev'ry nugget clean and sound,
Red's a jewel, smooth and round,
Worth a dollar'n ten a pound ;
Here's your gum, ye giddy girls,
    Here's your Maine spruce gum.
The chaps that went off with the Klondike
diggers
    For gold — jest gold,
Have slumped in the snow, and they work like
niggers,
    And they haven't got rich, we're told.
We're snowshoeing down from the north of
Katahdin,
    See here ! Yum, yum !
Here's a tole to tease Maud to come into the
garden
    —These rich, rosy lumps o' spruce gum.

———

Our fires are dowsed in the lonesome old camps,
We've left them to wolves and the foxes and
damps.
The trail of our snowshoes lies snakin' behind,
For we're clawing for home with the treasures
we've mined.
We've no sort of use for the pick and the sluice ;
Our Klondike has been the straight trunks of
the spruce.

Let them that elect grub the dirt for a "gleam,"
Our ore is the gum and our lode is the seam
That doesn't go sneaking in mire and clay,
But grins at the sun and drinks deep of broad day.

Go grope for your gold in the bowels of mud!
We'll cleave our fresh nuggets of resinous blood
Forced out from the heart through the fibre and
    vein
Of the giants who lurk in the woodlands of
    Maine.

Just squint through this bubble and gaze at the
    blaze:
That red is the fire of hot summer days;
That glimmer is autumn; that glow is the tint
That was lent by some campfire's guttering glint.
And here is a globe like the eye of a cat,
And this one is amber like honey; and that
Is a tear rosy red with the anger and shame
Of a king glooming down as the axe-heavers
    came;
— Staring down as around him his kin roared
    to earth
Midst the oaths of the swampers and Labor's
    rude mirth.
That tear of the spruce, may it go to the pearls
Flashing bright 'neath the lips of some sweetest
    of girls!

These, then, are the treasures we bring in our
   packs,
— Each round, rosy globule as sweet as the
   smacks
We'll get from the kids when they swoop with
   a roar
At dad just the second he opens the door.
Clear out your old scraps, Mr. Druggist: we
   come
With a good hefty jag of the season's new gum
      Ev'ry nugget clear and sound,
      Red's a jewel, smooth and round,
      Worth a dollar'n ten a pound.
      Here's your gum, ye giddy girls,
         Here's your Maine spruce gum.

REAR O' THE DRIVE

The rain has raised the river an' she's up to
    driving pitch,
An' it's oh, an' grab your peavies an' go sloppin'
    in the wet.
We've got ter send 'er whoopin' now without a
    ketch or hitch,
But it won't be kid-glove bus'ness, oh, my
        hearties, you can bet.
    Empty the water out of your boots
    And gaffle your peavies, you P.I. galoots.
There's the rips at Rundy's Corner, and the
    sluice at Puzzle Gorge ;
You can drive 'em and connive 'em, but the
    timber's bound to lodge.
An' sticks will buck — with best of luck — as
    offish-like as hogs,
For there ain't no calkerlatin' how you'll run a
    drive o' logs.

    Chase the heathen with a sword,
    Run the cattle with a goad,
All we want's our Oldtown peavies, when our
        drives go overboard.
    An' we'll foller, sloshin' in,
    Yes, we'll waller to the chin,
An' we'll herd 'em through the wildest stream
    that ever frothed and roared.

So, look alive,
It's after five,
An' the drouth is a-chasin' the rear o' the drive.

Foller down, foller down with your peavies on
   your backs,
For the herd that runs ahead of us goes loafin'
   'less it's chased.
They know they're off to market, an' they dread
   the saw an' axe,
An' you've got to go and welt 'em, though the
   water's to your waist,
For they balk on Depsconneagon when a sixty-
   footer halts ;
Ev'ry eddy stands a-ready for to swing 'em in a
   waltz.
An' ev'ry rock is chock-a-block with jack-strawed
   pine an' spruce,
Ontil you've got the devil's job to try and turn
   'em loose.

But our goadstick is the peavy, an' our cant-dog
   is the pup
That'll worry 'em an' hurry 'em an' rush 'em,
   chase 'em up.
Oh, the drouth is right behind us, but we've
   passed the North Twin flume,
An' we'll beat the sun in heaven in the race for
   Pea Cove boom.

MATIN SONG OF PETE LONG'S COOK

It's dark in the camp, and the woods outside
  Are dark, dark, too!
And a hundred men still open wide
  Their loud bay-zoo.
It's sort of mean to rout 'em jus'
  To work once more;
I'd like to let each tired cuss
  Jus' lay and snore.
But I've been up for an hour or two
  And grub's all on;
And now as the cook of Pete Long's crew
  I toot my horn.

————

The weirdest of all wood-sounds, by the way,
Is a cook's queer cadence at break of day:
          Whoo-e-e-e!
                    Git UP!
The grub is on the table, boys, the coffee's on
    the bile:
The swagon's hotter'n Tophet and I swear 'twill
    make you smile.
There's whiskers on the gingerbread, the biskit
    can't be beat;
I've got molasses sinkers made from mother's
    old receipt.

— Oh, I've got molasses sinkers built around
  some extra holes ;
They'll make you think of home and friends and
  tickle up your souls.
The beans come out a-roarin' when I boosted
  up the lid ;
They chuckled when I pried 'em out — they
  laughed, I swear they did.
Don't jolly me about your smells of Araby the
  blest,
— Jus' take a snuff of ground-baked beans all
  hot from out their nest.

The grub is on the table, boys, hurroop, hurroop,
  whoo-e-e-e !
Come, tumble out, git on a move ! Good Lord,
  it's after three !
Rise up and shine, my gentle lambs, surround
  your breakfast quick,
Or else you'll git the sun's ha-ha from over
  Tumble Dick.
And if the timer heaves a growl and docks you
  in his book,
Jus' blame your own durn lazy luck — don't
  lay it on the cook.
For ev'ry man who's et my cream-of-tartar bis-
  kit knows

The cook of this 'ere camp, by smut, 's the
    earliest bird that crows.
    For I'm old enough to spell a-a-a-ble!
    The grub is all on the ta-a-a-ble!
          Whoo-e-e-e!
             Git UP!

OFF FOR THE LUMBER WOODS

The duffle is packed, and the babies are smacked,
 and the wife has a buss and a hug ;
And she's done it up brown in a-loading me
 down with about all the grub I can lug,
   So long !   Good-by !
   I'm off !   Don't cry !
— Just about a month of Sundays and you'll
 see my homely mug.

———

Now look ye, ye towzled-haired son of a gun,
Be good to your mother or you'll see some
 fun
When your daddy comes down on the drive in
 the spring
And fetches a withe with a hornetty sting.
Ha ! ha ! you young rascal, you'd rather have
 gum ?
Well, be a good baby and pa'll fetch you some.

Yes, mother, you're right, it does seem kinder
 wrong
To leave you alone here the whole winter
 long.
And it's tough that I have to pack dunnage and
 break
For the big timber wrassle at Chamberlain lake.

But folks are a-waiting for lumber and boards,
They've picked up their saws, now they've laid
down their swords.
They're wanting the timbers for new city domes,
They're wanting the shingles for humble new
homes.
The hammers are waiting, the nails are on end,
And the chorus of clatter'll commence when we
send
A billion of lumber down race-way and sluice,
From the lonesome dominions of gloomy King
Spruce.
The men who print papers are wanting fresh
sheets,
The folks who build ships will be launching new
fleets,
For, mark me, no matter what Uncle Sam
planned,
He finds he can't reach his new back lots by
land.
Don't smile at me, wife, but I feel when I swing
That sweaty old axe from the fall to the spring,
That I hear one grim cry swimming up on the air
Through the dim, silent forest, — a pleading
prayer.
The clank of the press, and the scream of the
saws,
The grunt of the grinder that slavers and chaws

At the fibre of pulp wood; the purr of the plane
Are blent in one chorus, attuned to one strain,
— That sighs in the breezes or throbs in the roar
Of the tempest; and ever the cry is for " More."
And we men with our axes and horn-covered
    palms
Hear the call as a man hears the summons " To
    arms,"
And forward we plunge with no quarter, no
    truce,
With axes a-gleam in the realms of King Spruce.

The duffle is packed, and the babies are smacked;
    now wife, for a buss and a hug.
Save a smile 'gainst the spring, for I'm going to
    bring just all the spruce gum I can lug.
        I'm off!   Good-bye!
        So 'long!   Don't cry!
In about a month of Sundays you will see my
    homely mug.

HERE'S TO THE STOUT ASH POLE

Hooray for to-day, and hooray for to-night, and
    forget all the rest of it, boys.
Hold on, Mister Barkeeper, close up your jaw,
    we're paying for all of this noise.
We won't mosey out, and we won't set down,
    and you can't keep a one of us still;
You can charge, if you want to, so much for a
    yawp; we'll settle all right in the bill.
For this is our very last evenin' on earth; the
    last night we'll be here alive.
To-morrow at six we all cut sticks for the rear of
    the West Branch drive.
               Hooray!
For Seboomook, and rear of the drive.

Oh, bartender, say, can't you hustle them up?
    Come, push out your reddest of paint,
We're here for to splatter the carnation on, now
    blow us for fools if we ain't!
So set out your varnish for coffins, my boy, —
    that brand called the "Grave-diggers' Boast."
I've got enough chink — now down with your
    drink! and I'll give ye a riverman's toast.

While you're raising up your glasses,
Jest forget the giddy lasses

That have coaxed away your dollars, and have
    given you the laugh.
  Turn away from them connivers,
  And as honest, hearty drivers
Drink a good, round jorum to the stout ash staff.
  When the girls have filched your cash,
  There is still the hearty ash,
It is waiting at Seboomook for to cheer your
    foolish soul.
  Ah, you know we love it most; and I give
    you this, my toast,
The river driver's darling, oh, his long ash pole.

We've ridden the gorges on rioting logs, and
    we've always swept safe to the land.
So long as we rode with the spikes in our boots,
    and the long, limber pole in our hand;
We've pried at the jams on the brink of the
    dams, and the pole has stood by like a man,
And then in the dash for our lives in the crash
    the pole braced us up as we ran,
            Hooray!
As we yelled through the smother and ran.

And when in the bellow of up-ending logs it
    looked like good-by to our souls
We rode back to life from out of the strife,
    vaulting high on the end of our poles.

Ah, these are the friends that stand by you, my
    boys : they're truer than all of the host
Of the fair-spoken gang of the thieves of the
    town! Crowd up here and drink to my
    toast !

    The girls were sweeter'n honey
    Till they gathered in our money,
And the barkeeps they were pleasant just as
    long as we could spend.
    Now it's quite another story,
    — Case of throwdown ! But, by glory,
We can drink this final jorum to our stout old
    friend.
Though the gang has swiped our cash, there is
    still the hearty ash,
He is waiting at Seboomook for to cheer your
    foolish soul.
After all, we love him most ! and he's still the
    last, loud toast
— The driver's honest helper, oh, the long ash
    pole.

MISTER WHAT'S-HIS-NAME

OF SEBOOMOOK

Have you ever heard Seboomook with her April
    dander up,
    With the amber rushing river gorged to high-
    est drivin' pitch?
Have you heard her boom and bellow — rocky
    lips a-froth with yellow —
    When she spews and spumes the torrents —
    oh, the wild and wicked witch?

    She has menace in her breath,
    And she roars the chant of death,
For the victim that she slavers never sees
    the sun again.
    And she clutches at the river,
    With entreaty that it give her
The morsels for her longing, which are men —
    men — men!

Here's a tale to suit the cynic — 'tis a satire from
    the woods,
    And concerns a certain hero who was hunt-
    ing after Fame;
'Tis the grim and truthful story of a mighty
    reach for glory,
    But, alas, he didn't get it, for we've clean
    forgot his name!

He was one of Murphy's crew,
And he swore that he'd go through
Where no other West Branch driver ever saved
    the shirt he wore:
For he vowed he'd shoot the gorge
And allowed that he could dodge
The Death that knelt a-clutching at the prey
    the waters bore.

When they said he couldn't do it, why, he
    laughed the crowd to scorn,
  — Poled across the dimpling shallows with
  a fierce and hoarse good-by
— He was Murphy's top-notch driver, half a bird
  and one-half diver,
  But the best who brave Seboomook only
  sound the depths to die.

And they found him miles below;
But his mother would not know
The mangled mass Seboomook belched from out
    her vap'rous throat.
The first man coming down
Brought the story out to town,
Referring to the hero as a "dretful reckless
    goat."

Then he told the brisk reporters all the grim and
    grisly tale,
  And the deed was dressed in language in a
    way to bring some fame.
But alas for human glory, the galoot who brought
    the story,
  Remembered all the details, but forgot the
    fellow's name.

———

Have you ever heard Seboomook roaring at you
    in the night,
  With her champing jaws a-frothing in a word-
    less howl of hate?
'Tis a fierce vociferation to compel our admira-
    tion,
  For the chap who struck that rugged blow,
    cross-countered thus by Fate.

When he lunged his pole at Death,
When the river sucked his breath,
Seboomook gravely listened when he screamed
    his humble name;
  For the honor of a foe
  She would have the people know,
But she vainly dins her message in the deafened
    ear of Fame.

HA'NTS OF THE KINGDOM OF SPRUCE

The sheeted ghosts of moated grange
And misty wraiths are passing strange ;
The gibbering spooks and elfin freaks
And cackling witches' maudlin squeaks —

———

— They have terrified the nations, and have laid
the bravest low,
But intimidate a woodsman up in Maine? Why,
bless you, no!
Merely misty apparitions or some sad ancestral
spook
Serve to terrify a maiden or to warn a death-
marked duke.
But the P. I. scoffs their terrors, though he'll
never venture loose
'Mongst the ha'nts that roam the woodlands in
the weird domains of Spruce.
— He'll mock the fears of mystic and he'll scorn
the bookish tales
Of the fearsome apparitions of the past, but
courage fails
In the night when he awakens, all a-shiver in
his bunk,
And with ear against the logging hears the
steady, muffled thunk
Of the hairy fists of monsters, beating there in
grisly play,

— Horrid things that stroll o' night-times, never,
    never seen by day,
For he knows that though the spectres of the
    storied past are vain,
There is true and ghostly ravage in the forest
    depths of Maine.

———

For even in these days P. I.'s shake
At the great Swamp Swogon of Brassua Lake.
When it blitters and glabbers the long night
    through,
And shrieks for the souls of the shivering crew.
And all of us know of the witherlick
That prowls by the shore of the Cup-sup-tic.
Of the Side Hill Ranger whose eyeballs gleam
When the moon hangs gibbous over Abol
    stream;
— Of the Dolorous Demon that moans and calls
Through the mists of Abol-negassis falls.
And many a woodsman has felt his bunk
Tossed by the Phantom of Sourdna-hunk.
There's the Giant Spook who ha'nted Lane's
Old wangan camp and rended chains
— Great iron links of the snubbing cable —
As though they were straw — who was even
    able
To twist the links in a mighty mat
With which he bent the forest flat

From Nahma-kanta to Depsiconneag
— Acres and acres — league after league ;
Striding abroad from peak to dale
And laying on with his mighty flail.

Oh, fie for the shade of the manored hall,
A fig for a Thing in a grave-creased pall,
— For wraiths that flitter and flutter and sigh,
With flabby limbs and the sunken eye !
The woodsman recks not ye, frail ghosts,
But he knows and he bows to the deep wood's
    hosts,
Who sound their coming with giant breath,
Who mark their passing with storm and death,
Who shriek through blow-downs and howl o'er
    lakes,
— And he hides and trembles, he shivers and
    shakes
When he hears the Desperate Demons loose
In the weird dominions of grim King Spruce.

THE HERO OF THE COONSKIN CAP

When the blaze leaps forth from the camp's
    great hearth,
  And the fitful shadows come and go;
When the ruddy beam lights the deacon-seat
  And the silent faces in a row;
As the storm-gust drags at the sighing eaves
  And moans at the shuddering window-pane,
Some droning voice from a shadowy bank
  Intones a song to the wind's long strain,
And like the soughing, ebbing blast
  The gusty chorus bursts and swells;
And then one single, sighing voice
  Drones plaintively the tale it tells.
They're simple songs, they're homely songs,
  And yet they cling in heart and brain, ——
Those songs of the darkling forest depths,
  These songs of the lumber woods of Maine

There's the song of home and the song of love,
  And the lilt of battle, bold and free;
There's the song of the axe in the ringing wood,
  And the sighing song of the distant sea.
Yet oft when the choruses are stilled
  Some honest woodsman's voice can wake
A tender thrill with the homely song
  Of a nameless hero of Moosehead Lake.

A hero in leggings, he volunteered
   —When the treacherous ice lay black as loam
In the melting spring — to risk his life
   And bring to others the news from home.
He bore the mail for the lumber camp,
   The missives for many an anxious man
Who toiled for the ones he loved so well,
   In the wilds of the far Socatean.
He'd fingered each as he studied the names
   And sorted the letters with kindly care ;
While with honest heart of a friend he guessed
   At the news that the precious notes might
     bear.

There was one for Kane, and the last had said
   That his little girl was sorely ill —
Poor man, he had worried the whole long week !
   — And here was one for the Bluenose-Will,
Who had left a sweetheart to come to Maine,
   And had looked for a line in a homesick way ;
And here were a couple from Henry's wife,
   — And one bore " Forward without delay ! "
A tiny message to " Pa John Booth "
   Had a cross to show where a rousing smack
Had been pressed on the paper ; and here, alas,
   Was a letter fringed with a sombre black.
Freighted with sorrow or bringing the smiles,
   Fresh from the homes so far away,

He tucked them all in his coon-skin cap
   And breasted the sleet of the dreary day.
No one knew how it came about,
   No man witnessed the fight for breath,
When the cruel clutch of the great black lake
   Reached up and dragged him down to death.

But we always knew that his fiercest strength
   Was spent in the supreme flash of life
When he, poor wanderer, thought alone
   Of the news for others from home and wife.
For, as far on the edge of the broken ice
   As his arm could reach, when he sank and
     died,
We found the worn old coon-skin cap
   With the letters carefully tucked inside.

A HAIL TO THE HUNTER

Oh, we're getting under cover, for the "sport" is
    on the way,
— Pockets bulge with ammunition, and he's
    coming down to slay ;
All his cartridges are loaded and his trigger's on
    the "half,"
And he'll bore the thing that rustles, from a
    deer to Jersey calf.
He will shoot the foaming rapids, and he'll shoot
    the yearling bull.
And the farmer in the bushes — why, he'll fairly
    get pumped full.
For the gunner is in earnest, he is coming down
    to kill,
— Shoot you first and then inquire if he hurt
    you — yes, he will !
For the average city feller he has big game on
    the brain,
And imagines in October there is nothing else in
    Maine !
Therefore some absorbed old farmer cutting corn
    or pulling beans
Gets most mightily astonished with a bullet in
    his jeans.
So, O neighbor, scoot for cover or get out your
    armor plate,

— Johnnie's got his little rifle and is swooping
on the State.

Oh, we're learning, yes, we're learning, and I'll
warn you now, my son,

If you really mean to bore us you must bring a
bigger gun.

For the farmers have decided they will take no
further chance,

And progressive country merchants carry armor-
plated pants ;

— Carry shirts of chain-plate metal, lines of coats
all bullet-proof,

And the helmets they are selling beat a Knight
of Malta's " roof."

So I reckon that the farmers can proceed to get
their crops,

Yes, and chuckle while the bullet raps their
trouser seats and stops ;

And the hissing double-B shot as they criss-cross
over Maine

Will excite no more attention than the patter of
the rain.

And the calf will fly a signal and the Jersey
bull a sign,

And the horse a painted banner, reading " Hoss ;
Don't Shoot ; He's Mine ! "

And every fowl who wanders from the safety of
the pen

Will be taught to cackle shrilly, "Please don't
    plug me; I'm a hen."

Now with all these due precautions we are ready
    for the gang,
We'll endure the harmless tumult of the rifles'
    crack and bang,
For we're glad to have you with us — shoot the
    landscape full of holes;
We will back our brand-new armor for to save
    our precious souls.
O you feller in the city, those 'ere woods is full
    of fun,
We've got on our iron trousers — so come up
    and bring your gun!

HOSSES

THEM OLD RAZOOS AT TOPSHAM TRACK

Won't you poke your buzzin' stop-watch,
    Daddy Time, and click 'er back
To the days of spider high-wheels on the
    dinky Topsham track?
When they raced there in October for per-
    taters, corn, and oats —
Sometimes paid the purse in shotes —
Drivers wore their buff'ler coats,
And the weather was so juicy that the boys
    would take a vote
As to which would drag the better, suh, a sulky
    or a boat.
    Still 'twas fun, when the sun
    Got the moppin' bus'ness done,
And the field went off a-skatin', half the pelters
    on the run.
There was 'Liza, Old Keturah Ann, and Dough-
    nut Boy and Pat,
Their pedigrees was barnyard, but we didn't
    care for that;
So hooray! So hooroo! Oh, ye ought to see
    'em climb,
They was racers, suh, from 'way back — but no
    matter 'bout the time!
    There was goers in that pack —
    Look at Toggle-jointed Jack

With an action like a windmill, but the critter
      he could rack!
    And I'd like to have him back,
    For I tell you, bub, I stack
On the high-wheel, razoo-races of the good old
    Topsham track.

Oh, you oughter seen the send-offs, and you
    oughter seen the tricks!
For the stretch was chock-a-blocko when they
    scored 'em down by six.
And the starter he would whang-o on a dented
    strip of tin,
But the drivers never minded 'less he cussed the
    gang like sin.
The hoss-whips that they carried reached away
      beyond the manes,
    And they larruped 'em with chains —
    Tried to lift 'em by the reins.
'Twas muscle, suh, that won the race in them
    old days — not brains!
And you'd think to see the sawin' and the
    jerkin' and the h'ists,
The boys they was a-usin' partent webbin's
    made of j'ists.
Their elbows flapped like flyin' and they yow-
    wowed through the dust,
And 'twarn't through lack of hollerin' that ev'ry
    man warn't fust.

'Twas " Hi-i yah, cut the corners! " and " Hi-i
 yoop, take the pole! "
" Don't ye keep me in this pocket — let me out
 there, darn yer soul! "
" Gimme room there! don't ye pinch me or I'll
 bust yer blasted wheel! "
 " Hi, you sucker, that's a steal! "
 " That's a low-down trick, to squeal! "
" Oh, ye want some trouble, do ye? Wal, con-
 sarn yer harslet, peel! "
It was tetchy, mister, tetchy, to go sassin' on 'em
 back,
When the crowd got interested at the good old
 Topsham track.

There was Savage — Solly Savage — drivin'
 Adeline Success —
He had speed to sell at auction, but they bribed
 the cuss, I guess —
 For he pulled her tight and good —
 Pulled her settin' — then he stood.
Jest got up and braced his feet, suh, and he
 pulled her all he could.
But the blamed old mare was fussy, wasn't
 posted on the deal,
H'isted up her skeeter-duster and let out one
 mighty squeal.
She was leadin' of 'em easy on the back stretch
 at the turn,

And there wasn't no mistakin' that the race and
  heat were her'n.
  Ginger, ginger! She could go!
  When she didn't stub her toe,
Warn't a horse in all the county stood a show
  suh, stood a show!
Sol was madder'n snakes in hayin' — had a string
  of catnip fits,
Just unfastened both the traces and she hauled
  him by the bits.
  And that rank old Adeline
  She come snortin' 'crost the line
Least a dozen lengths a leader, and they soaked
  old Sol a fine.
Then the feller that had bribed him played tat-
  too on Solly's face,
And took back the dollar-fifty that he'd give him
  for the race;
But the boys they licked the feller. Solly got
  his money back,
For we stood for honest dealing at the good old
  Topsham track.

Now come join me, all old timers, — hip, hooray
  and tiger, too!
For the high-wheel days at Topsham and the
  good old-time razoo —
For the days of spider sulkies and the days of
  solid fun,

When we had a dozen knock-downs 'fore the
 race could be begun;
When 'twas "Huddup, Uncle Eli," and "H'
  along there, John, or bust;"
  And the man that finished fust,
  Though he argued and he cussed,
Might not always get decisions — 'twas accordin'
 to the dust;
And 'twas therefore kind of needful, suh, right
 after ev'ry heat,
To have another fight or so to settle who had
  beat;
  But they never left a grudge,
  Even when they licked the judge.
And we wasn't all teetotal, still we went it light
 on "budge,"
For we never took no stronger than some good
 New England rum —
Jest a mild and pleasant bev'rage — why, the
  deacons they took some!
  Then there wasn't pedigrees,
  And no chin-kerbumping knees,
And an av'rage field would manage jest to keep
 ahead the breeze.

But come join me, ye old-timers, in this pledge
 and one hurrah,
For the spanking, wide-hoofed pelters of the old
  days of "Hi yah-h-h,"

For a feller kinder feels
That he'd go without his meals
Jest to hear some more kiwhoopin' from the old-time trottin' spiels.
When the wind was in the drivers — nowadays it's in the wheels.
When the tang was in the weather on those autumn afternoons,
And the band got kind of dreamy in those good old-fashioned tunes.
Oh, 'twas awful good to set there on the sunny side the stand,
And to have your girl a-smilin' and a-snugglin', hand in hand ;
And to hear her, when you mentioned getting started pretty soon,
Whisper, blushin', "What's the hurry? There will be a lovely moon ! "
Ah, there's moisture on my eyelids and my voice is gettin' hoarse.
But 'tis prob'ly jest the mem'ry of the dust of that old course.
Oh, Daddy Time, if somehow you could only click your watch
And let a feller start again a race he's made a botch,
I wouldn't ask no better place to start my life anew

"With my arm behind her back, and a hidden, bashful smack
To sweeten all the pop-corn balls we munched at Topsham track."

Than on that stand that afternoon beside that
      girl I knew,
  With my arm behind her back,
  And a hidden, bashful smack
To sweeten all the popcorn balls we munched
  at Topsham track.

TO HIM WHO DRIV' THE STAGE

Here's a lyric for the man who's "druv' the
    stage,"
  For the hero of the webbin's and the whip;
Who has faced the wind and weather, fingers
    calloused by the leather,
    And in twenty years has never lost a trip.

Here's a tribute to the sway-back, spotted hoss,
  Who has struggled up the stony, gullied hills;
And his dorsal corrugations show the nature of
    his rations,
    — When he stops, he has to lean against the
    thills.

Here's obituary notice of the stage,
  Chief of hopeless and dilapidated wrecks;
With the cracked enamel awning, and its cush-
    ions ripped and yawning,
    And the body bumping down upon the "ex."

Here's alas and oh, the ancient "buff'ler robe,"
  With the baldness of a golden-wedding
    groom;
When the rain and snow descended, then some
    wondrous smells were blended,
    Till the stage was scented very like a tomb.

Here's a word for all the weary miles he
    ploughed,
  When the drifts had piled the stage-road
    mountain high,
When the night shut down around him and the
    north wind sought and found him,
  And the tempest chilled his blood and blurred
    his eye.

There were only country letters in the bags,
  And the bags were lank, and yet his word was
    " Must."
And he felt as if the nation knew his fierce
    determination
  That he'd have the mail sacks through on time
    or bust.

Here's rebuke to those contractors who have
    skinned
  The stipends of our Uncle Sam's star routes,
Till the men who drive the stages hardly get
    enough in wages
  To keep their little shavers' feet in boots.

Here's a lyric, then, for him who drives the stage;
  When you ride behind his ragged back, don't
    frown,
But endure the bang and slamming, for the
    man who's earned the damning
  Is the contract-sharp who bid the wages down.

HE BACKED A BLAMED OLD HORSE

The neighbors came a-nosing 'round and said the
    horse could trot
— He oughter up and killed him then, right
    there upon the spot;
A-killed him, yas, and tanned his hide and made
    it into boots,
Then worn 'em out a-kicking 'round them neigh-
    borly galoots
Who set the bee to buzzing under Ezry Booker's
    hat,
And filled him up and chucked him full of non-
    sense such as that
He'd got a hoss 'twas bound to make his ever-
    lasting pile,
And what he got to do, of course, was handle
    him in style;
That he must bandage up his legs and figger on
    his feed,
And give him reg'lar exercise and work him out
    for speed.
His knees, his neck, his breast, his thighs, the
    way he lugged his head,
And all his other symptoms looked to " speed,"
    the neighbors said.
So Ezry he just sucked it in, as child-like as
    could be,

—It cost him thirteen dollars to look up the pedigree.

Then one day down to Laneses store he ribbled off a mess

Of names that struck your Uncle Dud as so much foolishness.

"I've traced him back," so Ezry said, "to Morgan blood 'nd Drew,"

To what's-his-name and this and that, and which and t'other, too.

And Ezry banged the counter, just excited as could be,

A-arguing out the knots and kinks in that there pedigree.

Land sakes! He couldn't seem to think of nothing but that plug:

— Neglected work, let slide his farm, went crazy as a bug.

But there! The neighbors stood around and said to go ahead,

And Ezra like a blamed old fool just swallowed all they said.

Ef they'd turned to and burned his barn 'twould been a prison crime,

But 'twould have been a better thing for Ezry ev'ry time.

He could have got insurance then, but 'twas a total loss

When they torched Ezry up to back
    A Blamed
        Old
            Hoss!

Of course he had to put that horse in some good
    trainer's hands,
And trainers, as the man who's tried deereckly
    understands,
Ain't driving just to take the air, for scenery or
    for health,
But sort of grab a feller's leg and milk him for
    his wealth.
And there were blankets, straps, and girths, and
    bandages and boots;
Pnoomatic sulkies, pads, and shoes, and hoods
    and stable suits;
And lotions, too, and liniments — the best of
    hay and oats,
And Lord knows what of this and that for trot-
    ters' backs and throats!
Then came the entrance fees, of course, and
    travelling expense,
For Ezry lugged that trotter round, and didn't
    have the sense
To know when he was fairly licked, but always
    would persist
That "that air hoss another year is going in the
    list!"

The trainer said he'd have him there; the neigh-
bors thought so, too;
So Ezry pulled his pocketbook and said he'd see
him through.
So 'round the circuit went the hoss and, though
'tis sad to tell,
"The Flying Dutchman" didn't fly — he never
got a smell.
And when he'd come a-puffing in behind the
whole blamed crowd
Then Ezry swore and shook his fist, and argued
'round, and vowed
That all the rest was down on him and had,
without a doubt,
Just pooled together in a scheme to shut The
Dutchman out.
The driver said so, anyway, and then, you know,
a few
Good neighbors took him out one side and said
they thought so too.
And so — but land, it's plain enough how Ezry's
money went
— He wound up his race-hoss career without a
blasted cent.
What's more, he ain't the only one who's sunk
his little pot
In fubbing 'round from track to track with
horses that can't trot.

— He ain't the only man in Maine whose ever-
    lasting curse
Has been some darn-fool neighbors, and his itch
    to win a purse.
And, as I've said, if they'd turned to, and burnt
    his barn instead
Of cracking up that hoss so much and turning
    Ezry's head,
He could have got insurance then, but 'twas a
    total loss
When they torched Ezry up to back
        A Blamed
            Old
                Hoss!

B. BROWN — HOSS ORATOR

I've heerd of Demosthenes — b'longed down in
    Greece,
  — And Cicero, too!
  But 'course, never knew
A great deal about 'em except through my niece,
Who's tended the 'cademy, — lets on to know
'Bout most of the critters who lived years ago,
— Who'd talk to a standstill the chaps of their
    day
With a broadside of words like a gatling, they
    say.
And folks knuckle down, and praise up, and
    kow-tow
To those hefty old tongue-lashing chaps even
    now.
So I'm ready for brickbats, and hollers, and howls,
From the folks of the schools, and from hide-
    bound old owls,
When I shin the high flag-staff of Fame to tear
    down
All colors that flop there for rival renown,
And string up the banner of Bennington Brown.

  Don't think I'll assert
  What he knew ever hurt!
  He was mostly considered an ornery squirt.

He traded old hosses, and cattle, and such,
And the sayin' 'round town was : " Oh, Brown,
    he ain't much ! "
But I read t'other day, in a volyum called
    " Hints,"
That a speaker is gauged by his gifts to convince.
So I stand on that statement and solemnly swear
That as a star-actor convincer, I'd dare
Back Bennington Brown up against the best
    man
That ever tongue wrassled, grab holts, catch as
    can.
Give Cicero Pointer, Directum, or Hanks,
And Brown an old pelter with wobbly shanks,
— Just leave 'em an hour, no odds, a clear field,
No matter how Cicero sputtered and spieled,
I'll bet he would find himself talked to a stop,
And Brown would unload the old rip, even swap !

    I can see how he'd look
    When he carefully took
    Old Cic by the gallus with " come-along " hook
Of that gnurly forefinger. And there Cic would
    stand,
For he wouldn't be yankin' away from that hand,
Unless in his desperate efforts to skip
Cic dodged from his toga, and gave Brown the
    slip.

And it's likely that Brown would talk something
    like this :

" I ain't at all anxious to shift with you, Cic.

Your hoss, I'll admit, has got plenty of speed,

But you know, Cic, you know that he ain't what
    you need.

Outside of a show piece to stand in the barn,

That hoss he ain't worth, Cic, a tinker's gol-
    darn.

What you want is that hoss of mine — want him
    blame bad,

He don't need no whip, crackers, cudgel, or gad.

'Thout strap, boot, or toeweights, he's gone out
    and showed

His quarters in thirty. He stands lots of road,

And I swow I dunno what I'm sellin' him for,

— I need him myself. But I'll sell! Have a
    chaw ?

And as I was sayin', he's just what you want ; —

Oh, yes, have to own he's a leetle dite gaunt !

Been a-drivin' him hard, for he'll stand lots of
    work,

Never had a sick day, never shows the least
    quirk.

He's young : look yourself ; jest you roll up his
    lip ;

By the way, ever smile ? I've some stuff on my
    hip.

Now as I was sayin'"— and on, and so on,
Till Cicero'd put his suspenders in pawn,
Hand over his steed for a wind-broken brute,
And sling in some golden sestertia to boot.

 I tell you again,
 That of all of the men
 Who can slat the King's English, I swear by
  old Ben !
And you'll never appreciate half of my praise
Till you've stood there yourself in the beller
 and blaze
Of his thirteen-inch barker, and fust thing you
 know
Discover you've bought an old bone yard or so,
I hardly expect, O ye hurrying throng,
Ye'll bow to my hero, applaud my rude song,
But sling, if ye will, all your bouquets and praise
At the cut-and-dried speakers of pod-auger days,
I'll go by myself and I'll tenderly crown
With bay the bald brows of old Bennington
 Brown.

"JEST A LIFT"

Feller was far as the foot of the hill in one of
    those boggy places,
  Had a first-class team,
  As strong as a beam,
But the feller had busted his traces;
And the feller gave up when he saw he was
    stuck.
He borrowed a chaw and consarned his luck,
— Admitted he didn't know what to do;
Sat down on a bank and looked so blue
He worried the people that passed, and they
Just turned their noses the other way.
Old Ammi Simmons muttered that he
Was a dite afraid of his whiffle-tree;
It was slivered some, "and there warn't much
    doubt
'Twould bust if he pulled that feller out."
And Ira Dorsey, regretful and smug,
Would have helped had he brought his heavier
    tug,
So he simply beamed a bright " good day "
And clucked to his team and rode away.
So thus they passed for an hour or two;
Many not noticing, while a few
Assured him they'd like to help him out
"If the rigging they had was only stout."

Feller had thought he was up a stump, when
    along drove Ivory Keller;
  Saw the sunken hub,
  Yelled, "What's the troub?
Don't ye want a lift there, feller?"
And the feller said that he did, you bet,
But said he had begged while he'd set and set,
And he hadn't discovered a single man
Who'd give him a boost with an extra span.
"Why," Ivory said, "that's jest my holt.
That off hoss there ain't more'n a colt,
And it's hardly an extry pulling pair,
But it's yourn for what it's worth, I swear.
For I've got a home-made sort of a rule
— Won't kick a cripple nor sass a fool,
And when I find that a feller's stuck
— A side-tracked chap down on his luck —
Why, bless you, neighbor, in jest about
Two shakes of a sheep's tail I yank him out."
And the very next thing that the feller knew
Old Ivory busted a chain or two,
But the horse and the colt and the gay old man
Bent to the job till the clogged wheels ran,
— Tugged and buckled with hearty will
Till the cart rolled over the tough old hill.
Then the feller begged him to take some pay,
But the old man chuckled and shoved him
    away;

" Why, bub, see here," said Ivory Keller,
" I'm a tollable busy son of a gun,
And this is the way I squeeze in fun,
— Grab in same's this and help a feller."

BART OF BRIGHTON

'Tis the tale of Bart of Brighton — meaning
    Brighton up in Maine ;
  It's the tale of Uncle Bart, sir, and his racker-
    gaited mare ;
I have toned it down a little where the language
    was profane,
  But the rest is as he told it — this remarkable
    affair.
  It is very wrong to swear ;
  Bart admits the fact — but there!
Times occur when human nature simply is
    obliged to " r'ar."

———

" It's all along o' givin' lifts to Uncle Isr'el
    Clark,
— His folks don't like him stubbin' round the
    village after dark, —
And old Mis' Clark has asked of folks that see
    him on the road
To take him in and bring him home, if 'tain't too
    much a load.
The day this 'ere affair come off I'd took in
    Uncle Pease,
With a pail of new molasses that he hugged be-
    tween his knees.
We see old Clark ahead of us, a-lugging home
    a gun.

Says I to Pease, 'Now brace yer hat: we'll have
a leetle fun.'
'Set in behind, old Clark,' I says. 'Hop in behind,' says I.
'Prowidin' these 'ere tugs don't bust I'll take
you like a fly.'
He piled aboard, s'r, master quick, there warn't
no need to tease,
And there he sot, the gun straight up, the butt
between his knees.

"I'll tell you 'bout that mare of mine — the
more you holler 'whoa,'
I've larnt the whelp to clench her teeth, and
h'ist her tail — and go!
And when we got clus' down to Clark's I thought
for jest a sell
I'd make believe we'd run away. So I com-
menced to yell,
And old man Pease he hugged his knees and
gaffled to his pail.
And now, my boy, purraps you think that turn-
out didn't sail!
He hugged his gun, did Uncle Clark, and set and
hollered 'Oh!'
While I kep' nudgin' Uncle Pease and bellered,
'Durn ye, whoa!'

"I larfed, suh, like a lunytick, I larfed and
thought 'twas fun

To look around and see old Clark a-hangin' to
his gun,

For he was scart plum nigh to death, and so was
Uncle Pease,

Who doubled clus' above that pail he clenched
between his knees.

But while I larfed I clean forgot the Jackson
corderoy,

And when we struck that on the run, we got
our h'ist, my boy.

Old Clark went up jest like a ball and, next the
critter knowed,

Come whizzlin' down, s'r, gun and all, starn-
fust there in the road.

And when the gun-butt struck the ground, ker-
whango, off she went,

— Both barrels of her, all to onct, and then —
wal, 'twas — hell-bent!

The off-rein bust, the wheels r'ared up — the old
mare give a heave,

That runaway was on for sure — there warn't
no make-believe;

With t'other rein I geed the mare up-hill to'ards
Clarkses yard,

— We struck the doorstep, struck her fair, and
struck her mighty hard!

And long as Lord shall give me breath I shan't
forget the eye
That old Aunt Clark shot out at me as we went
whoopin' by.
Then I went out and Pease went out and things
got kinder blue
— 'Twas sev'ral minits by the clock 'fore this
old cock come to.
And there the old mare'd climbed the fence and
stood inside the gate,
With eyes stuck out and ears stuck back and
head and tail up straight.
And from the way she looked at me 'twas master
evident
She wasn't catchin' on to what this celebration
meant.
And I was clutchin' jest about two feet of one
the reins,
While Uncle Pease was dodderin' round, a-yellin'
' Blood and brains ! '
For, bless my soul, when he had lit he'd run
himself head-fust
Right down in that molasses pail ; — he thought
his head had bust !
And that the stuff a-runnin' down and gobbed
acrost his face
Was quarts of gore, and so old Pease had clean
give up his case.

And there he stood like some old hen a-drippin'
    in the rain,
And hollered stiddy, 'Blood and brain, I'm
    dead ; oh, blood and brain!'
Old Uncle Clark was on his back, a-listening to
    the fuss,
And wonderin' whuther that old gun had
    murdered him or us.

" Now that's the way the thing come off. Best
    is," concluded Bart,
" They warn't nobody hurt a mite : three-fifty
    fixed the cart."
But as he spoke he sought to hide a poultice
    with his hat
And curtly said, " Oh, jest a tunk! you see,
    Aunt Clark done that."

———

'Tis the tale of Bart of Brighton — mean-
    ing Brighton up in Maine,
    — It's the tale of Uncle Bart, sir, and his
    racker-gaited mare ;
I have toned it down a little where the language
    was profane,
    But the rest is as he told it, this remarkable
    affair.

GOIN' T' SCHOOL

THE PAIL I LUGGED TO SCHOOL

I know my confession is homely, but Yankees
    are Yankees clean through,
Their dollars make shells like a turtle's, but
    their hearts, my dear fellow, are true
To the dear, sacred days of their childhood, and
    luxury loses its charm :
— The only good things are the old things to
    the fellow brought up on the farm.
And I'd trade all the cheer of a banquet, I'd
    "swop" them, as grandpap would say,
For the tang of the infinite gusto that came to
    me, when, after play,
I lifted the battered tin cover and squared my
    brown arms to assail
The grub that this hearty young shaver had
    carried to school in his pail.

God bless her, that darling old mother! She
    cherished the honest conceit
That the groundwork of boyish good morals is,
    first of all, plenty to eat.
And though I went barefoot in summer, with
    trousers cut over from Jim's,
We scampered to school every morning with
    dinner pails filled to their brims.

There were doughnuts, both holed ones and
    twisters, and always a bottle of cream,
And jell cakes and tarts and all such like — oh,
    how the kids' eyes used to gleam!
I pitied the poor little shavers who slunk to a
    corner to eat,
Who brought only bread and potatoes and never
    had anything sweet;
And some carried grub in their pockets, and hid
    with a child's bitter shame
To choke down the crust and the cooky before
    some rude fun-maker came.
But out of such manhood's successes of which
    I've a right to be proud
There never was one I've uncovered, with such
    a delight, to the crowd
As that pail with its bountiful dinner, each
    cake and each jelly-tipped tart
A dumb but an eloquent voucher of a thoughtful
    and true mother-heart.
And, neighbors, from things I have noted, I
    think it's a pretty good rule
To size up a mother's devotion by the grub her
    child carries to school.
Those savors that float from my childhood dull
    all the delights of my board;
The good things from mother's old kitchen my
    dollars can never afford,

And I'd trade all these delicate dishes — a clean
   unconditional sale —
For the tang of the infinite gusto from the depths
   of that old dinner pail.

THE PADDYWHACKS

Mother says it's something fearful — way this
    pesky young one acts,
And she's called the Johnson children by the
    name of " Paddywhacks."
And she keeps a-givin' orders that I musn't have
    'em round;
But she thinks that Satan's in me, for she says
    I'm always bound
To go mixing with 'em somehow when she lets
    me out to play;
And you bet I'm going to see 'em if I have to
    run away.
    I'll never wear them blamed dude clothes
    Nor boots with patent leather toes.
    I like to stomp and scnff and kick
    And holler round.   It makes me sick
    To have that Reynolds youngster call,
    He's primped up like a big wax doll.
    My mother says he's just too sweet,
    He always keeps his clothes so neat,
    And wishes I'd spruce up a bit.
    What!   Look like that?   Well, I guess nit!
    — They've dirty mugs and ragged backs,
    But just give me them Paddywhacks.

They can catch ye lots of suckers — know the
    brook and shortest cut;
They have got a robber's dungeon and a nice
    browse Injun hut.
They can scrape ye lots of slyver — juicy stuff
    from little pines,
They can make a willow whistle, and they're
    posted on the signs
Of woodchucks, coons, and squirrels; and they
    own a brindle houn',
And they get to going barefoot first of any boys
    in town.
    That's the stuff — oh, that's the stuff,
    Let a kid kick up and scuff!
    Not go round with mouth all screwed
    Goody, like that Reynolds dude.
    Say, I'll push him once, if he
    Comes a-making mouths at me.
    Yah, yah! See them corkscrew curls!
    That's right, let him play with girls.
    Let him wear his ruffled shirt
    — Give me one that won't show dirt.
    I'm the chap, you bet, that stacks
    Up 'long-side them Paddywhacks.

THAT MAYBASKET FOR MABEL FRY

Mother rigged the little basket, for I'd teased a
　　day or so,
— I was just a little shaver, and 'twas years and
　　years ago, —
And I blushed while I was teasing; I was young,
　　so mother said,
To be running 'round with baskets when I ought
　　to be in bed.
But she trimmed me up the basket and she asked
　　me whom 'twas for;
Ah, I didn't dare to tell her; thought I'd better
　　hold my jaw,
For I wanted it for Mabel, not for Minnie on the
　　Hill;
— For a maid in rags and tatters, not a maid in
　　lace and frill.
Minnie rode behind her ponies; Mabel had a
　　wooden cart,
But to Mabel went the homage of my foolish
　　boyish heart.
True, her gown was frayed and ragged, and her
　　folks were sort of low,
And her brothers swore like demons, and they
　　tagged where'er we'd go,
And my father always scolded me and drove
　　them all away

"And the dearest affection the heart can hold
Is the honest love of a five-year-old."

Whene'er they followed Mabel if I asked her up
    to play.
But I saw not Mabel's tatters; for I loved her
    sun-browned face,
And I'd lick the kid that didn't say she was the
       handsomest girl in the place.
    'Tis a tricksy prank that memory plays
    Taking me back to those early days;
    But the purest affection the heart can hold
    Is the honest love of a nine-year-old.
    It isn't checked by the five-barred gate
    Of worldly prudence and real estate.
    And that, my friend, was the reason why
    I hung my basket to Mabel Fry,
    She'd a tattered dress, and a pink great toe
    Stuck out through her shoe, but — I loved
      her so —
    Though that was years and years ago.

I sat down and looked at mother while she
    trimmed the pasteboard box,
While she crimped the crinkly paper till it fluffed
    like curly locks;
Till she fastened on the streamers, red and
    yellow, white and blue,
And she held it up and twirled it, saying, " Sonny,
    will that do ? "

Would it do? It was a beauty! 'Twas a gem
  in basket art;
And I piled it full of candy, put on top a big
  red heart.
Then as soon as dusk could hide me I escaped
  my mother's eyes,
And I hung the grand creation on the door-latch
  of the Frys.
How my youthful limbs were shaking! how my
  dizzy noddle rocked!
And my heart was pounding louder than my
  knuckles when I knocked.
So she caught me at the corner, for you see I
  didn't fly,
— Might have been I was so frightened; then
  perhaps I didn't try.
When I swung around to meet her, neither of
  us dared to stir.
Mabel stood and watched the sidewalk and I
  stood and gawked at her,
While those little imps of brothers gobbled every
  blessed mite
Of the candy in that basket — Mabel didn't get a
  bite.
But I saved the little basket, gave each kid a
  hearty cuff,
And I tried to comfort Mabel; told her she was
  sweet enough,

— Said she didn't need the candy; but my little
  Mabel sighed,
Blushed and whispered that she wondered how
       I knew — I hadn't tried —
    To-day — to-day from a long-gone May
    This tricksy memory strays my way.
    Just for a moment I close my eyes
    And see that cracked old door of Fry's.
    And my heart is brushed, as the noon day
      trees
    Are touched with the whisp of the strolling
      breeze.
    Alas, that the heart mayn't always hold
    The honest love of the nine-year-old.
    I haven't a doubt you're dreaming now
    Of some frank maid with an honest brow
    Who chose you out for she loved you so,
    When Worth got " Yes," and Wealth got
      " No."
    But that was years and years ago.

THE MYSTIC BAND

I've joined the orders that came our way,
— Been sort of a " jiner," as one would say, —
And I've bucked the goat, and trudged the sands,
And taken the oaths in most secret bands,
Till now at last I seldom slip
On test or password, sign or grip.
And every day when I walk the street
I give the signs to the men I meet.
There's the S. of T. and the K. of P.
And the League of the Order of Liberty;
Masons and Odd Fellows string along,
Thicker than flies in the moving throng.
Till it seems that every fellow could
Give you a sign of a brotherhood.
Oh, I like to meet them, every one,
From the Daughter of Peace to a Son of a Gun.
But I can't quite feel the same delight
As I used to when, some summer night,
I'd take a few of the high degrees
In the O. K. K. B. W. P's.

We had no lodge-room with locks and bars
— Our hall was the dome 'neath the winking
  stars ;
No lofty dais and tufted throne,
No crown or symbol or altar stone,

No velvet carpets or flashing lights
Were needed there in those old-time rites;
There was only the light from some honest eyes
Up-raised to the velvet evening skies;
And the only crown was the flower wreath
Set light on the curling locks beneath,
And the mystic grip was the tender squeeze
Of our hands as we roamed past the orchard
   trees;
And the head of the lodge was an elfin chap
With roses heaped in his dimpled lap.
— With wings a-spread and his locks a-blow,
And the wand of his office a silver bow.
He welcomed the timid neophytes.
And into the hearts of his pure delights
He led each happy candidate
Who breathed Love's password at the gate,
And happy he who sought degrees
In the O. K. K. B. W. P's.

'Tis just a page from the dear conceit
That makes the volume of school life sweet;
— A bit of a jest from the callow days
When we bashfully trudged the self-same ways
As the girls from the evening meeting took,
And we carried their capes and the singing-book.
— Sauntered along the dim old lanes
With chirrup and chatter and gay refrains,

Shouting " Good-nights " as here and there,
Pausing by gate or stile, a pair
Loitered a bit on the threshold's stone
For a sweet and fond good-night of their own.
It irks me, friend, that I must profane
The oath of the order and voice that chain
Of mystic letters : yet 'twere not kind
To take you thus far and leave you blind.

And I'll whisper, you know, just heart to heart,
'Twas " One Kind Kiss Before We Part,"
The mystic grip was a warm hand-press,
The sign and the test a swift caress,
And the dearest and sweetest of Used-to-be's
Were the O. K. K. B. W. P's.

AT THE OLD "GOOL"

"Ten, ten and a double ten, forty-five and then
    fifteen!"
Stand you here, old friend of mine, close your
    eyes the while you lean
Your silvered hair against the wood that's silvered
    too, by sun and rain,
— The butt of storms as well as we, — old aliens
    crawling back to Maine.
The driving sleet, the drifting snows have filched
    away the vivid red
That matched, as I remember it, the flaming top-
    knot on your head.
And this — so gaunt, so bent, so small — it seems,
    alas, a wooden ghost
Of what it was when it was "gool" : the school-
    house's old red hitching-post!
And ah, old friend, to lean your brow upon its
    crest you have to stoop;
— You had to stretch to reach its top in those
    old days of hide-and-coop.
  "Ten, ten and a double ten,"
  That's the way we counted then;
  — Counted hundreds rapidly,
  Begged the happy days to flee.
  Moments were not precious then.
  What we hoard to-day as men,

Then we flung in careless way;
Counting life as when at play;
" Blinding " at the old red post,
We strove to see who'd count the most.
" Forty-five and then fifteen, — "
Lavish then : ah, now we glean
On our bended knees as men
What we flung uncounted then.
Friend, old friend, the past troops back
With all its smiles and all its sighs,
    When I was "It,"
    And the world was lit
By the star-shine of two soft brown eyes.

" Ten, ten, and a double ten, forty-five and then
    fifteen ! "
That talisman of boyhood days has brought a
    sorrow that is keen.
And yet there's joy along with pain ; let me bow
    my head here too,
And here with brow upon this wood I'll tell you
    what you never knew.
You've asked me many times, old friend, the
    secret of an unwed life ;
I'll tell you now : I loved but once ; that girl
    loved you ; she was your wife.
I loved her in those boyhood days, but in Life's
    game of counting out

Fate's happy finger stretched to you, and I —
    poor awkward, bashful lout —
Just stepped aside. But 'twas all right! I'm
    not the sort to curse and whine,
My joy has been that she was yours, so long as
    she could not be mine.
— My joy, old friend, is now to say, as here we
    clasp this worn old post,
There is no heart-burn in my past, no shimmer of
    a jealous ghost.
For boyhood's lesson taught me this : 'Tis only
    some egregious fool
Who rails at Fate and storms the skies because
    some better man " tags gool."
I've been content to stand there, friend, while
    one by one the eager troop
Of boyhood's chums have won their goal in Life's
    more earnest hide-and-coop.
Thank God, old chum, we still clasp hands and
    pledge again our boyhood ties.
    Though I've been " It,"
    And your world is lit
By the star-shine of her soft brown eyes.